Also by J. Krishnamurti

Life Ahead
Education and the Significance of Life
On Education
Think on These Things
Talks with American Students
The Whole Movement of Life is Learning

Unconditioning and Education

The need for a radical approach

J. Krishnamurti

Volume 1

Dialogues with parents, teachers and trustees
in Malibu and Ojai, California

KFA
Krishnamurti Foundation of America

Unconditioning and Education Volume 1
The Need for a Radical Approach

J. Krishnamurti (1895–1986)

Edited by Ray McCoy and Duncan Toms

ISBN: 1517401062
ISBN: 9781517401061

Krishnamurti Foundation Trust Ltd
Brockwood Park
Bramdean, Alresford, Hampshire, SO24 0LQ
England

Published by Krishnamurti Foundation of America

Krishnamurti Foundation of America
PO Box 1560
Ojai, California, 93024
USA

The official repository of the authentic teachings of J. Krishnamurti:
www.jkrishnamurti.org

From ancient days, man has sought something beyond the materialistic world, something immeasurable, something sacred. It is the intent of this school to inquire into this possibility.

This whole movement of inquiry into knowledge, into oneself, into the possibility of something beyond knowledge, brings about naturally a psychological revolution, and from this comes, inevitably, a totally different order in human relationships, which is society. The intelligent understanding of all this can bring about a profound change in the consciousness of mankind.

J. Krishnamurti,
The Intent of the Oak Grove School

CONTENTS

FOREWORD

In the lifetime of J. Krishnamurti, the last school that began with his help was in the town of Ojai in California. He had first spent time there in 1922 and, after 1933, stayed the longest continuous periods of his life in the valley. Since the early 1930s, large numbers of people had attended his public talks in the town; families moved there because of their interest in what he said. It was in Ojai that he wrote his first major book, *Education and the Significance of Life*, published in 1953. The possibility of starting a school in his name had been mentioned from time to time after 1953, but there was no concerted movement for it until friends who had formed the Krishnamurti Foundation of America began serious discussions with him about his views on right education.

In 1970, in one of his recorded conversations with himself, Krishnamurti asked:

> Could not the intelligent minority of parents get together and start a school in which the whole of man is considered and cared for, in which the educator is not merely the informant, a machine which imparts knowledge, but is concerned with the well-being of the whole human being? ... It means creating a place where the educator is being educated, and the help of a few parents who are deeply interested. (*From Beginnings of Learning, first published by Victor Gollancz Ltd in 1975.*)

It may have been with this in mind that Krishnamurti agreed to meet with some trustees of KFA and other friends, first in Malibu in 1974, and continuing with parents, trustees and prospective teachers in Ojai in 1975, to discuss starting a school. The two volumes of *Unconditioning and Education* present these remarkable dialogues, which led to the opening of Oak Grove School in 1976.

Krishnamurti begins the discussions by explaining that traditional education prepares children to conform to society, to memorize facts in order to acquire knowledge. He says that this limits the mind by narrowing its function and limiting its creativity. The educators and the children are conditioned to traditional patterns of inquiry, neglecting exploration of broader development as whole human beings psychologically, spiritually, intellectually and morally. He would have the educators explore the possibility of bringing about a different kind of mind.

Krishnamurti asks the bold question: 'Is there a method to uncondition the human mind?' He suggests that the conditioning of tradition and society can be 'uncovered and dissolved'. He wants the parents to be involved in this, to understand the intention that, in talking with their children, walking with them, living with them, the parents, the teachers and the children will establish a relationship in which there is no authority, but a sense of freedom to explore and to grow inwardly. Then when the children leave the school they will have good minds that are intelligent, 'can meet any challenge and understand what it means to be religious'.

Krishnamurti's great vision of true education is expressed in his statement about the intent of Oak Grove School:

The whole movement of inquiry into knowledge, into oneself, into the possibility of something beyond knowledge, brings about naturally a psychological revolution, and from this comes, inevitably, a totally different order in human relationships, which is society. The intelligent understanding of all this can bring about a profound change in the consciousness of mankind.

The Editors

INTRODUCTION

Why are we being educated at all?
J. Krishnamurti interviewed by Fred Hall

Mr Fred Hall (FH): Mr Krishnamurti, you are now working toward the realisation of a new school in the Ojai Valley, an educational centre. We have, I think, four or five private schools and an abundance of public schools here. Now, I'm wondering why another school.

Krishnamurti (K): You are asking what the difference is between this school and other schools.

FH: Certainly.

K: Sir, first of all, why are we being educated at all? When we are educated, in public schools, private schools, universities and colleges and so on, either we condition the mind or we give emphasis to a particular segment of the brain, which is the cultivation of memory and the skill in action of that memory. That is what is generally considered education in the modern world, both in Europe and in America. And it is going on in India. All that is a fragmentary kind of education. What we are trying to do is to educate the whole of man.

FH: Will you be starting with a very young child in elementary school?

K: Yes, from the age of 8 to 18.

FH: Would you require any particular background for this youngster?

K: No, no. Naturally, we do not want them to be drug addicts, (Laughs) and when children's parents are divorced, it makes it awfully difficult.

FH: You do not want a disturbed child.

K: We can have one or two, but not a whole group of them.

FH: Are you talking of a residential school?

K: Residential as well as partly non-residential.

FH: And you would offer a basic education of the kind that is required.

K: Of course, first class academically, as we do in England and India.

FH: Well now, just in reading some notes about the school, you refer to it as a place where one can learn a way of living that is whole, sane, and holy. Would you mind taking those three things, whole, sane, and holy, and explaining to me what you mean?

K: You see, the word *whole*, if you look in a good dictionary, means healthy, physically healthy. That means, non-drug, non-alcohol, non-smoking and keeping the body perfectly healthy. The right nutrition, good food, all that is implied. Then, *sane*; that word *sanity* means a mind that is not crippled by belief, a mind that is not conditioned by propaganda, that is capable of thinking clearly, freely, not bound to any particular tradition.

FH: Are any of us at 8 years of age, for example, in that position?

K: Of course not, poor chaps! No, of course not, but as they progress, as they grow older, we are going to work to have a right relationship between the teacher and the student, so that in discussing with them, both the teacher and the student uncondition themselves. That is the whole problem of education.

And *whole* means, also, holy: to treat life as something sacred. After all, man is not just an animal and not just a technological entity. We want to respect nature. We want to respect other human beings, not become violent, not become brutal, selfish. All that is implied in that word *holy*, and much more.

FH: Do you see a tendency today in school systems throughout the world to dwell on material things primarily, how to function in society?

K: Oh, obviously. Because everybody is concerned with how to get money, get a job, get a position—in India as well.

FH: They are all trying to make their way.

K: They are all trying that, and therefore it is becoming very materialistic, though they pretend to be very spiritual—you know: 'I believe in this', and another believes in that. That is all pretence, it is make-believe; actually all of them are going after money.

FH: What is the net result of this kind of education?

K: Well, you see, it is accepting immoral governments, irresponsible action; accepting violence and immorality as a natural thing. And if it is not that, it is drugs or alcohol, or sex which is another form of drug, and is rampant. You know what is happening in this country, and it is gradually, unfortunately, spreading all over the world.

FH: America is the instigator?

K: I'm afraid so, and also America, especially California, has set an example in certain other things, not just freedom and inquiry. You know all that.

FH: You talk of a school as a place where one learns both the importance of knowledge and its irrelevance. Explain its irrelevance.

K: Sir, what is the function of knowledge? What is the function of accumulated experience technologically, scientifically, sociologically? It becomes knowledge, stored up in the brain as a remembrance which will help you to act skilfully. That is the function of knowledge, and if we function only in that realm we are merely becoming computers, which we are.

FH: We have no life of our own.

K: Through thousands of years our brains have become excellent computers; not as good as electronic computers, but we function automatically, mechanically, superficially. One realises the superficiality of a mechanical way of living, a repetitive way of living, a second-hand way of living. All knowledge is second-hand. A man may have new knowledge, but it becomes second-hand the next minute. If you live in that there is actually no freedom. It is like having an excellent computer and talking about freedom. It is irrelevant. And you must have freedom to learn, you must have freedom to inquire. I mean, the whole Christian world as well as the Hindus and Muslims are conditioned to certain forms of belief, dogma, rituals, tradition. And so gradually what should be human inquiry into truth becomes an acceptance of faith or a belief or a dogma, or constant repetition of rituals. I feel knowledge has its place. It must have its place, otherwise we could not do all this, but as long as we remain in that area all our life there are other areas which we neglect totally, which are slowly beginning to awaken.

FH: Are they beginning to awaken because of an awareness that we are missing these things?

K: No, I think the awakening is because there is a great deal of mystery involved in it, a great deal of mythology, a great sense that this is so limited that we must find something else.

Unfortunately, it is not from understanding when knowledge is irrelevant and when it is relevant.

FH: If you take a youngster who is about 8 years old who has grown up in an average family, and has been conditioned by the prejudices and biases of...

K: ...the society he lives in, by the friends he has. The other day we were talking to a boy of 15 or 14; he is already becoming violent.

FH: How do you remove him or separate him from that kind of conditioning?

K: If he comes to a school of this kind it is our responsibility, the educator's responsibility, to see that, in discussing with the student and in having lessons and all that, both the teacher and the student see that they are conditioned. It is not that I am unconditioned and you are conditioned, but that we are both conditioned, so let us—through talk, through discussion, through watching, through observing ourselves, through all kinds of methods—uncondition ourselves. Because otherwise we destroy each other; that is what is happening in the world.

FH: Of course. So your choice of teacher is really the key, isn't it? It must be extremely difficult to recruit.

K: Of course, extremely difficult. Because, in the world, an educator is ill-paid, is not respected, and those who cannot get good jobs turn up to be teachers.

FH: And those who have good jobs become cautious and very conservative.

K: So we have tremendous difficulty in finding the right teachers.

FH: How are you going about it at the present time?

K: We are doing it by asking whoever is interested to come and stay with us, discuss it, go into it, see what we can do. It isn't for money. Of course, you have to have money to live and so on. Primarily it is to bring about a different relationship between human beings, between the educator and the educated.

FH: Let's stop for just a moment and talk about the physical entity that will be this school. Where will it be and how might it begin, in terms of buildings and so on?

K: Sir, you know the Oak Grove, down there.

FH: Where you talk from time to time.

K: We have that property now, about one hundred acres.

FH: One hundred of the most beautiful acres in the world, I think.

K: I know. They are enchanted by that. It is high up; it's like a nest. The whole town along with Meiners Oaks and all those hideous buildings, but on top there it is completely like a new world. We've been there with the architect, and have more or less chosen the places with him. And we need money, you know, the whole business.

FH: Oh sure. As I understand it, money derived from your talks here this year will go toward that school.

K: Ah, no, I personally do not take money at all. I have no bank account. I have a horror of all that stuff. I'm not a guru who is coining money and hoarding it up. (Laughs) They need money, are asking people for donations, begging, passing the hat around.

FH: You'll start in a small way, then.

K: Obviously, small and slowly, carefully. We are not going to have 500 students right off. We cannot. We will probably start with 30 or 20.

FH: Will it be more than a school, will it be a meeting place, a place to meditate?

K: Yes. That is why we have called it the educational centre; a place where older people can come to think, discuss, exchange, meditate, go into things, go into themselves, transform. It is not just a meeting place, it is a very serious thing.

FH: Is it similar at all to the school at Brockwood Park in England?

K: Yes and no. (Laughs) There are four schools in India which I helped to start—I am not boasting about it, I am just helping to start. Each school should be different from the others, not just imitate, so that it is a creative thing. Brockwood is entirely different from the Indian schools; and we want this school in Ojai to be entirely different from the others. But they all have the characteristic that they are international, that they are non-authoritarian, non-hierarchical, not the principal first and then the students. We are creating it all together, with the parents who take interest in the school, who come there, look at it, discuss it with us. It is a total thing; it is not we start it and everybody else looks on. The parents, the teachers, the older people who are interested in all this, all of us are creating this.

FH: I had wanted to ask you about the parents because that's a third factor: students, teachers, parents.

K: Yes, parents. We have suggested that the parents should take part in all this. And the parents want their children to be educated this way, not educated one way at school and at home be pushed in another direction. That would put the poor child in a great conflict. So, there must be cooperation from the teachers, from the students, from the parents.

FH: And from the community to some extent.

K: The community, if they wish to join, may come into it.

FH: I would like to ask you about three more words, in the context of your views of them. If I may quote this little pamphlet, you say, 'It is here one learns the importance of relationship which is not based on attachment or possessiveness. It is in the school one must learn about the movement of thought, love and death, for all this is the whole of life'. Thought, love, death.

K: Yes. (Laughs)

FH: We talked a little about thought, less about love and death, I think.

K: Yes. You see, sir, it is a very complex subject. The whole Western world—for the moment I am talking about that; but I am not contrasting it with the Eastern world. The Western world is based on thought. Their religion is based on thought.

FH: To some extent.

K: They invent the mysterious. Thought invents the saviour. Thought invents all the structure of religion and all the economic relationships. They call it love but it is essentially based on thought. I am not saying it is right or wrong, I am pointing out. With the result that one lives a totally contradictory life. You believe in morality and act immorally. It is so obvious what has happened in America during the last few years with the whole business of politics. The Eastern world said thought cannot possibly capture or understand the immeasurable, because thought is fragmented, thought is limited, finite, and through thought you cannot understand reality, nor truth, and so on. But they exercise thought to capture that. They said to control thought, meditate, force your body, do this, don't do that, follow your guru, all that nonsense. So both are the same. But we are saying thought has its right place, but thought cannot possibly understand *the other*. So you have to find energy—I am sorry to use simple words—to find energy that will not be created by thought. Say, for instance, thought creates the energy of competition, thought creates the energy of possession: 'I possess my house, my wife', and so the energy that thought creates breeds conflict. These are all facts, not my invention. If you will observe it, you will see that when you are attached, you become the house.

FH: That holds the thoughts.

K: Of course. If I am attached to a piece of furniture, I become that furniture; I am that furniture. If I possess my wife, as most men do, what am I possessing? It is the idea of my wife, or my girl or whatever it is, or my boy, the image I have created about her or him, that I possess.

FH: Yes, I do follow you. And you talk of thought as being finite. Love is infinite then?

K: No, we must understand what love is. Is love pleasure? We have made it sexual pleasure. We have made love of the earth a pleasure. But is love pleasure? Pleasure means memory; that is, I had a marvellous experience and I recorded it; the brain records it, and that gives me great pleasure, and I want to repeat it.

FH: So I love it.

K: I love it.

FH: Yes.

K: So, one has to find what love is. Is love pleasure, fulfilment, desire? Can a man who is ambitious love?

FH: That is a good question.

K: Can a man who is competitive love? He might say, 'I love you, my darling', to his wife or his girl, but on the side he is ambitious, competitive, aggressive, violent. So love can only exist when there is not this sense of an ambitious, competitive, aggressive, violent mind.

FH: The third word: death.

K: Ah, death. Oh yes. (Laughs) Do you want to talk seriously about it?

FH: In the time that we have, yes. You said very clearly here, and I imagine that many people reading this, having heard you many times, would know what you meant.

K: I will tell you what I mean. Sir, the ancient Egyptians believed in reincarnation. In India and in Asia they believe in that, believe that they are going to be reborn in a next life. The reward in a next life or the punishment in a next life depends on what you do now, how you behave, because behaviour is the highest form of relationship between man and man. If you do not behave properly you are going to pay for it next. They do not behave, but they believe in reincarnation, which is nonsense. And in the Christian world they have their own ideas of resurrection.

FH: And of heaven and hell.

K: If you do not believe in Jesus, you go to hell; if you do not accept certain dogmas, you go to hell. The Christian world, with the inquisition, with excommunication, with threats; all that is part of fear. On one hand you say, 'Love Jesus', and on the other hand you say, 'If you do not believe, you will go to hell'. It is all so utterly irrational and stupid. So one has to find out, without believing, what happens when you die. Will one find out what death means in a state of unconsciousness or disease? Or you have an accident and are killed? Or in creeping old age when you become gaga, senile, and say, 'Oh my God, I am frightened of death'? When you are diseased, unconscious, you cannot find out anything. So, what is the significance? The organism does not go on forever and ever, because we misuse it, we drink too much, we indulge in too much sex, so we destroy the organism. It has its own intelligence, but to find out what death means psychologi-cally—it means really to be free of all that you have: your name, your wife, your house, your money, your everything. That is going to happen to you. Now, can you voluntarily be free of all that, in living? So that you incarnate each day, make yourself anew.

FH: I see. You talk of the death of the conditioned self.

K: No, death of the self, not the conditioned self. Self is condi-tioned, is the result of conditioning.

FH: Yes, yes. There is one other basic question I have to ask you that is a kind of all-encompassing one. You have travelled far and spoken often and have been heard by millions, and you have created several schools and another now in the off-ing. Do you feel that you have made a dent, that you've com-municated meaningfully with large numbers of people?

K: I hope so, sir.

FH: Do you feel that it is worth the effort?

K: I would do it even if it was not, if it had no results. I don't seek a result; that is a horror. This is what I want to say; take it or leave it. This is real; face it. It is a thing that everyone has to face. You have to face this life. You have to act righteously now. Because otherwise we are destroying everything. We are destroying the whales. We are destroying the earth. The com-munists, the Christians have destroyed people by the millions. I say, for God's sake listen to what I am saying; do not accept it or deny it; just look.

FH: Do we delude ourselves entirely when we feel that we have become civilised?

K: I question it. Are we evolving only in the sense of becom-ing more inwardly concerned with life, not with just getting money, cars, position? Otherwise, what is the point of all this?

What's the point of killing people in the name of nationality or God, or whatever?

FH: Young people increasingly seem to be asking that question. Is that encouraging to you?

K: Yes, sir, but they won't stick to it. You see what is happening in America. All these gurus are creating such havoc in this country, bringing their old, conditioned beliefs and theories and dogmas. It is just the same as the Christian world.

FH: Why are they getting such an acceptance?

K: Because Americans want something new.

FH: A new answer, because the old one doesn't work?

K: But the new answer is clothed in different words and they think it's marvellous, romantic. You are told not to drink or not to have sex or to believe in Krishna, all that business, and it is amusing for a little while, but they soon give that up and go after something else.

FH: So, really, we are talking about this sort of approach to understanding. It is no more important than an attachment to rock music, for example.

K: It is the same thing. Whether you are attached to rock music or attached to an image or attached to a belief, it is exactly the same thing.

FH: How far are you along in recruiting teachers and is there any deadline or goal for starting?

K: We will start with two teachers or one teacher, with five boys or girls. That is enough.

FH: And an elementary school in the beginning. Are you looking toward a higher...

K: Perhaps later on. We have to see how things go.

FH: What has been your experience in other countries? Have you extended into the upper grades there?

K: Oh, college and so on.

FH: Have they been going long enough that you have any kind of conclusions?

K: You see, sir, when we started in India, for example, we started with nothing. We slept on the ground, went to bed with the sun, got up with the sun, because there was no electricity, no lamps. We started very quietly, so-called primitively, with the very young, and gradually it has grown into one of the best schools in India. But that is still not sufficient. And at Brockwood there are about 55 students only. We do not want more. And there are thirteen nationalities there; no authority, and so on. So, you see, the difficulty is that the world is too much. The world has become so appalling. I do not know if you know all that is going on. The parents, especially in India, want the students to earn their own livelihood, to have a job, get married and settle down and be safe. And you know what that implies.

FH: We're back to conformity.

K: Conformity, imitation, acceptance of things as they are. 'Don't create trouble. Trouble is there, but don't add more to it. Swallow it and stay with it, and follow the tradition that is in India. Accept authority. Parents are right'. If they say become an engineer, you become an engineer. They say, 'Follow the parents; they know better than you do'. And here and in Europe they say, 'To hell with all that. We want to do what we think is right'. And they go off at a tangent. They must, because they are inexperienced; they don't know. They suffer, they see the misery all around them, they say, 'I don't want to belong to all this mess', but they create their own mess.

FH: Is there any one country you could single out that perhaps is superior to others?

K: No, I'm afraid not, sir. I have travelled in Australia and in India, all over Europe, but it is all so messy. The politicians are not helping. The religious people are not helping; they are not religious really; they only call themselves religious. You know, sir, Buddhism in the ancient days and partly Hinduism, never went to war. They said do not kill. Now, I have never eaten meat in my life nor smoked. I was brought up as a Brahmin. I never touch meat. In India their tradition is not to kill, but now they have forgotten all that, so they kill. They eat meat. This misery is spreading, all around. In England and in Europe, the immediate demands must be satisfied; 'Do not bother with tomorrow or what is going to happen'. You know all this, sir.

FH: Yes, I certainly follow the news and am involved in covering it and of course I see it. You sound very pessimistic when I talk to you, but I don't think you are.

K: No, I am not pessimistic. On the contrary. But these are facts. This is what is going on. You must face it, not cover it up and say it is the fault of the politicians, the fault of the priests. It is your responsibility, each person's responsibility for creating this horror.

FH: In a democracy such as we have, are there greater opportunities for correcting?

K: Greater opportunities and greater corruption.

FH: Is there any way the community here can help now toward the beginning of the school?

K: Yes, sir, take interest, be responsible, find out, help to build it, help to give money. If I am interested in something, I will be part of the circus. (Laughs) I think we become irresponsible by saying it is the fault of somebody else, that the politician or politics will change, and will solve all of our problems. Of course not. Our problems lie much deeper in ourselves.

FH: We can hope there are a few political leaders because of the power they wield may have some recognition of that. Do you think that there are?

K: I have talked to many politicians, I have talked to cabinet members. Once they get into power, something happens to them. They are decent people, incorruptible, nice, friendly; the moment they get into a position, something happens to them.

FH: I want to wish you a great deal of luck in your new venture here, and we will be looking forward to your talks.

1

THROUGH A DIFFERENT KIND OF EDUCATION A NEW HUMAN BEING COMES INTO BEING

Krishnamurti (K): In what way are these schools in England and in India different from other schools? What is it we want to do in these schools? What is the relationship of this school in America, in Ojai, California, to the rest of the world and to the American community? We ought to look at the present situation in America, and from there go on to find out what kind of school we want, what kind of relationship this school will have with the American culture, if there is an American culture, and in what way this school is different from ordinary public and private schools.

Please do not think I am talking against America, I am not. I have been in this country since 1922, fifty-two years ago. I have travelled a bit in America, so I am not in any way opposed to the beautiful country and the really very nice, generous people, but we ought to consider the present situation.

The totalitarian governments, China and Russia with all its satellites, are impregnably authoritarian, and their sense of order is to live according to a dead ideology. You must know all this; I am just repeating it so that we are familiar with our phraseologies and our means of verbal communication. Europe, where I have travelled considerably and talked with many people, is not very creative.

You come to America and you see an extraordinary sense of disorder, politically, religiously, morally, sexually; in every way there is disorder; and there is no new culture being born here, as far as I see it. I may be mistaken, so please correct me if I am. There is no new creative impulse, except technologically. Technologically, the know-how of Americans is extraordinary and is spreading all over the world. Commercialism and consumerism are taking the place of culture; and you know what is happening politically. The religious spirit does not exist in this country—or anywhere else as far as I am concerned. The new gurus who come to this country are really horrendous; money, power, position have become extraordinarily important to these wretched gurus. They have nothing to tell people except to bring the old dead tradition of India. You must know all this; I am just telling you what is probably very obvious. Democracy as opposed to totalitarianism seems so shoddy, irresponsible, permissive and without any sense of order.

If we are going to create, bring about or form a new school, what are the children, the students being educated for? Are we educating them to be like the rest—disorderly, immoral, utterly without any sense of culture and decency? I am sorry to speak rather strongly, because I feel rather strongly about this. Are we going to educate them to conform to all the vulgarity that is going on: commercialism, consumerism, a sense of utter superficiality?

So what is the intention of all of us? Because it is not K's school; it is our school. At least, I feel that way. To me, a personal school according to my ideas will be dead. This is our school, yours, mine, and the parents' and the students'. What is it we are trying to do? How are we to educate the students and therefore ourselves to be a totally different kind of human being? That is really the issue. The present human beings, apart from a few exceptions, are savages, barbarians. I'm using the word *barbarian* in the right sense of that word. Do we want to make the students conform to a pattern or to make them into glorified clerks, business people, technicians? Can we educate to help them to live in this world and not withdraw from the world? What is it we want to do?

If one had a son or a daughter or were a teacher of those children, what kind of education would I want them to have? I like my children, I love them, but I have no time. I have to go and earn money. And I quarrel with my wife about my personal problems opposed to her personal problems, and she has to go and earn in a career and we have very little time for the children. Therefore there is no love, no sense of companionship, affection, confidence. The children grow up wild and become like the rest of the world. We are going to start a school at Ojai, so what is our responsibility?

In what way are we responsible, and to whom? To the parents? To the society in which we live? To the children? Or to ourselves? Or to a concept we have of what the children should be? What is my responsibility if I am a teacher at the school in Ojai? To whom am I responsible—to the ideas, to the words, to the intimation of K's teachings? If I am responsible to that teaching then I have become totally irresponsible.

Because then I am responsible to a concept of what I think the teachings are and I try to conform my concepts or my ideas, or lack of ideas, to what he has to say. Therefore I become irresponsible. As long as I am conforming to a concept, I am not responsible. The concept becomes responsible. So that is one point.

Then, am I responsible to what I feel, what I think, to what I think education should be? And what do I think? And how do I know what I think is true? Is it an opinion, an evaluation of an observation of what is going on around me? I draw a conclusion from that, and that becomes my fixed opinion. Am I responsible to that opinion, or am I responsible to the parents?

The parents, do they care for their children? Have they time? Am I responsible to them? And what do they want? In India the parents want the children to pass examinations, to get a degree, to get a job, get married and settle down and rot for the rest of their life. In Europe, again the same problem: job, position, physical security, and so on. And here, what do the parents want? Do they care enough or love their children enough to see that they have a different kind of education, that they flower into a different kind of human being who is not everlastingly commercially-minded, in competition, vulgar, superficial, seeking pleasure at any cost? Am I responsible to the parents who are inclined that way?

See what is happening in the world, not only in America, in Europe, Russia, China, India and so on. Have a total observation of what is actually going on. See the confusion, the misery, the suffering, the agony that all the parents are going through: the wars, the violence, the brutality. Seeing all that, not according to our opinions and judgements but seeing exactly as it is, from that observation can we together bring about a different kind of education so that the student or the children become really intelligent? That word, from *inter-legere*, means to read between the lines; and much more than that of course. It really means, for me at least, sensitivity, living a life in which there is no conflict, living a really tremendously austere life inwardly. Austerity means generally: severity, harshness, as the austerity of the monk which denies beauty, affection, love, tenderness. I don't mean austerity in that sense. Intelligence also means the capacity to think very clearly, objectively, not personally, not emotionally, sentimentally, romantically. And that intelligence comes into being when there is perception and action. Perceiving is the doing. All that is implied in that word.

Now, can we together at a school in Ojai bring about an atmosphere of freedom? Not permissiveness to do what each one wants to do, but a sense, an atmosphere of freedom, order, virtue. Can we bring that about in the school we are going to begin? That is, the students will have to know lots of technological things and at the same time cultivate a freedom which is not always operating in the field of knowledge. Look at what is happening in India, Russia, China, Europe and America. They are cultivating knowledge; they are cultivating memory extensively, gathering tremendous information in all the fields of science, mathematics, geography, history and so on, and they are not even concerned with the rest of the field of existence.

We must have knowledge, mathematics, history and all that, so how can we cultivate knowledge on the one hand and also bring about in the very act of teaching a freedom from it? Because otherwise we will never be creative, we will merely expand the field of knowledge, in the world of art, science and so on; innovation rather than creation. After all, art has become that, something new, innovative; they are always expanding and contriving to change the shape of the new, of the known, and that is not creativeness. At least I see it that way; I may be wrong. To be really creative means to be free, psychologically, inwardly, tremendously free from all kinds of things. This is not the moment to go into that. Out of freedom comes creative flowering, not only in the world of technology and art but spiritually, inwardly. Can this be done in the school: cultivate knowledge and at the same time bring about freedom from knowledge? And both of them operating harmoniously together in the field of living.

To put it differently, we are second-hand human beings, and being second-hand we can never be creative. Being second-hand we must always live in the prison of knowledge, and that knowledge is becoming more and more important, more and more enslaving, more and more demanding so that human beings can live and survive in that field. And nobody is concerned with the other fields. On the contrary, the other fields become very dangerous to the field of knowledge—at least they think so. So that is our problem more or less; I have put it very crudely and rather insufficiently, but we can go into it a great deal, in detail.

Say I am a teacher in a school in India, in England or here. I know mathematics means order. Is anybody here a mathematician? Sir, you know very well what it means. Mathematics means order, not merely numerals, not merely the learning that two and two make four, but the whole sense of tremendous order. Now, how am I to convey to the student not only the necessity of learning mathematics as order but also teach him, help him to learn what order means in himself and outwardly in his action?

Look, sirs, I am a teacher at Ojai. I have students before me, about ten of them, and I want to convey to them first, not mathematics, not learning two and two makes four and so on, but I want to convey to them what order means in life. Because without order there is no security. The brain can function only when it has complete security. It may seek that security in neurotic habits, neurotic ideas and so on, but it must have order, which is security. Now, I want to convey this to them; that is my first job. As a mathematics teacher, that is my first job. How am I going to convey the sense of great inward and outward order? Because I am disorderly inwardly. I am contradictory, I am messy, and the students who come from a messy home have already been contaminated by society, already have all kinds of fanciful ideas: 'Why should I obey you?' and so on. So how am I as a teacher, confused, disorderly in myself, to do this, knowing the student is disorderly and confused and obstinate and, like modern American children, disrespectful, yelling, shouting?

I know they must know mathematics. It is good for the brain. The brain is meant to be used in many ways, so they must know mathematics. That's my secondary problem, the teaching of mathematics. We'll come to that presently, how to teach. In front of these ten students I am greatly concerned that they should live in order. I don't know what it means because I am disorderly, I am confused, but I know the importance, the necessity, the essentiality of living in order. Because then the brain is absolutely clear, because it is completely secure. Now, how shall I do this?

Questioner (Q): Mustn't you make the children feel secure so that their brains can operate efficiently?

K: How do you make the brain of a child secure?

Q: First, you are warm and you create an atmosphere in which there is no fear.

K: That means you must have a residential school.

Q: Not necessarily.

K: Just see, sir. I will show you why. We have done this in India. They go off to their homes. They feel insecure there because the parents are tired, bored, insulted. The parents come home tired and have very little time for the children. Then the children come to the teachers and for a few hours they feel secure, if you can manage it. See what has happened: insecure at home, secure at school. Right? So what is happening in them?

Q: Conflict.

K: Yes. So how will you prevent this?

Q: Can you talk about the structure of this conflict?

K: We will.

Q: No, no, I'm not asking you, but can one talk about this and help the students to understand this?

K: If they are reasonable. If you can reason with them.

Q: Yes, but this is very difficult to do this with a 6 year old, you see? Because he doesn't have sophistication, and he is dependent. He must be dependent on your approval, on your love, on your warmth, on your guidance.

K: Of course. So how will you arrange or manage this?

Q: Well, this means that you must not only deal with the child, you must deal with the parents and the teachers.

K: What does that mean? Go into it, sir. You talk to the parents. You say, 'Look, you have to have time for your children, you have to cultivate confidence in them towards you. You must have affection, care, love'. Right? And have they?

Q: Maybe, maybe not.

K: Have they actually? Not maybe, maybe not; because in America both of them are earning a livelihood. They must leave the house at eight or nine or whatever it is, and come back at five or six, tired out. So what shall we do? I think we will come to that question a little later; we will find an answer to that. Either a residential school...

Q: Or at least a school where there are no barriers between home and school.

K: That means the parents must live in the school.

Q: Or must feel responsibility that they are the school.

K: I am not objecting to anything that you are saying, but to feel responsible they must have time. They don't have time. That is why all these children are behaving as they are; they have no love at home. Love means something entirely different: to see that they are educated properly, that they do not go out to kill animals, kill nature, kill people. All that is implied. And the parents are not interested in all that, except for very, very few. We will come back to this.

My responsibility towards the students is that they should know as much as they can in the field of knowledge, and also come to a kind of inward freedom. In that atmosphere I want us to grow; myself and them. I want to teach mathematics; and mathematics is order. But I am disorderly: I smoke, I drink, I do all kinds of contradictory things. I tell the children not to smoke, and I smoke. I am in contradiction myself, and the students are in contradiction in themselves. So how shall I who live in disorder talk to them about order? I become a hypocrite, and they smell that very quickly. So what shall I do?

Q: We need to investigate without condemning this disorder within ourselves.

K: But I am a teacher. I have taken the responsibility of teaching. See my difficulty. Shall I wait till I have cleared up my disorder? By then I am an old man. (Laughter) So what shall I do in my relationship to the students?

Q: Perhaps if one becomes very honest with one's students.

K: Do investigate a little bit more. I am a teacher. I live in disorder and the students are in disorder. I say order is necessary. How shall I bring this about, both in the student and myself? Knowing both of us, the student and myself, live in disorder, are confused, miserable and all the rest of it, how shall I deal with this problem? If I were a teacher, I know what I would do. I would talk to them first, not about mathematics. I would say, 'Look, you live in disorder, I live in disorder. We are both living in a world of disorder'. So what does that do when I acknowledge that I am in disorder and they are in disorder? What then is our relationship with each other?

Q: There is no separation.

K: No, there is the sense of communion, no sense of inequality, no sense superior and inferior. I am not the teacher laying down the law. So I talk to them. I say, 'Look, I am in disorder and you are in disorder. We are both going to learn through disorder what order is'. So we are learning. Not from me; we are both in the act of learning. So I talk about learning. What is learning? I am learning from myself in relationship to you, how disorderly my life is. You as a student are learning from observing how your life is disorderly. Both of us are learning. I am not telling you what order is. The communists will tell you what order is, as dictatorships throughout the world have done, as the religions have done, which are another form of dictatorship, but here I tell them, 'Look, you and I are going to learn by looking into disorder'. I cannot learn what order is without knowing what disorder is. So I go into that. What is disorder? Is order to do what one likes?

Q: Evidently not.

K: No, not *evidently*—I must be clear and they must be clear, because we both are learning.

Q: Yes, but you can see it and you can show it to them. When Jimmy wants this toy and Billy wants this toy and they are at each other's throats, that is disorder.

K: So, what? So order means not doing what you like.

Q: Of course not.

K: Wait, sir, see what is implied in it. Are you telling me that I can never do what I want to do?

Q: No.

K: Sir, don't say no. My whole social, psychological urge is to do what I want to do. Every advertisement says to do what you want to do. Yes? The whole of commercialism is based on that. It is not so easy. So I have tell them. I go into it. In that way I am clearing my own confusion. So I learn about what it is to act without always projecting what I want to do. It is a very complex problem; it cannot be settled in forty-five minutes in a class. Every day I am going to go at it. Before the mathematics class begins, I talk about this, put it in ten different ways: what does order at home mean? Obeying the parents? What does obedience mean? Why do you obey at all? I go into it day after day, day after day. They get the feeling of it more than through words because I am clearing up my own disorder by talking about it with them. It is an interrelationship. Then, after doing that for five minutes or ten minutes, I begin mathematics. Then it has a meaning.

So my responsibility becomes enormous, not only with regard to creating the atmosphere, which includes environment, but also in the class, an atmosphere of seriousness. Because without that quality of seriousness you can't learn. I am using the word *learn* not merely in the field of knowledge but also to learn about oneself, about the world, about everything. So I am a serious person. Apart from being a teacher in a school—for myself I am speaking—I am a very serious person and I want to convey this to them, that life is serious, not something to play around till you die, have a jolly good time. I am serious so I have to convey this to them. That implies how I behave. If I say something I mean it. All that is involved in it. No contradiction in myself. But I am contradiction, so I have to create this atmosphere in which both of us are learning. And that is the educational centre—you follow?—for grownups, for young children, that we are there to learn, from each other. That's one problem.

And also order means discipline. Not the discipline of the military, not the discipline of suppression, control, obedience to authority. Can there be discipline in freedom? In the school, freedom is essential otherwise you cannot create; we become like machines, as America is doing now. There is no freedom. They are vulgar. Sorry, you are all Americans, forgive me. They are pursuing whatever somebody tells them, one fad after another fad. So can there be freedom and order? And what is discipline? The word *discipline* means to learn. Now, can I learn and so be highly disciplined? Can I learn about discipline and so be disciplined?

I learn mathematics. In the very learning of it there is a certain discipline. Every craft has its own discipline. If I am to be a good gardener, the very learning about gardening brings its own discipline—not imposed, not suppressed, not controlled, but as I am learning about gardening I am seeing. So can I as a teacher at the school in Ojai convey this sense of discipline and order—without authority, without obedience, without conformity? Which means without fear. Can I as a teacher bring a discipline in which none of these exist? Freedom implies no authority, doesn't it? Obviously. And what has happened in America? There is no authority; therefore permissiveness, do what you want to do. And politically what is happening?

So what is discipline? A school must have that.

Q: Doesn't discipline involve learning for the sake of learning, plus a sense of responsibility?

K: I don't quite know what you mean by 'for the sake of learning'.

Q: Well, you're not working at something because you want to get my approval. You are intensely absorbed in it, and there is no discipline, no learning. There is just your absorption.

K: Yes, which means what, sir? Watch it carefully. When you are absorbed by a toy, is that discipline?

Q: It carries with it a certain discipline.

K: Go into it a little bit. I'm not saying you are right or wrong. I am absorbed by this, it's a marvellous toy. The toy absorbs me. Jesus absorbs me. (Laughs) That is another toy. Or Zen or this or that absorbs me and I think I am very orderly. Is it order when something outside of me absorbs me? I see that mountain. It is a marvellous thing to see a lovely mountain. The beauty of it completely knocks me out and I am absorbed by it. And when that is not, I am back into my naughtiness, my ugliness, my stupidity. See the danger of it, sir. I am not saying you are right or wrong.

So what is discipline?

Q: When I am learning, there seems to be a dialogue that goes on, a back and forth process. I look at something, and then there's some work that's involved also. So I might look at mathematics and I see something, I see the beauty of it, and there is also a process of working with it.

K: Yes, sir, I understand that.

Q: It seems there is a different quality in that than just being knocked out, by the beauty of something.

K: Quite.

Now, you see, the children have to be punctual. How will you help them to be punctual? Without fear, without conformity, without obedience, punishment, reward and all the rest of it, how will you make them punctual? I am coming to the practical. How will you do it?

Q: Be punctual oneself first.

K: Understood. And you tell the boy, 'Be punctual', ten times; and ten times he is not punctual. How will you cultivate it, how will you help him to want to be punctual?

Q: Well, if there is something interesting going on then...

K: No, no, that means something outside forcing him to be punctual.

Q: Not necessarily. If one is doing what is interesting because one is truly interested...

K: No, wait. He may not be punctual for meals—how will you make him?

Q: It seems the first thing is to find out why he is not punctual.

K: All right. Go into it, sir. See the difficulty. Bearing in mind: freedom, no authority and therefore no fear, no punishment; and yet he must be punctual, must have the desire to be punctual, the feeling that he must be punctual. How will you create this in him?

Q: Doesn't it mean that you are at a certain place at a certain time for something? You then don't just run by the clock. There is a reason to be punctual.

K: Sir, the food is ready at one o'clock. The cook has prepared it. If the students are not punctual the food gets cold, and the cook gets bored with it. So, how will you create the consideration in the student to be punctual?

Q: If you have an intense interest in that child and you want to look with his eyes, you work it out with him what is going on, what the problem is. You have to look, be aware of what is going on with him.

K: I understand that. That is simple, clear. Now move a step further.

Q: You must let him know the effects of his actions.

K: That is punishment.

Q: No, no, it's not punishment if you say, 'Look at the cook. She prepared that meal. She did all that'.

K: Yes, you talk to him. You talk to him about punctuality beforehand. He has to be there at one, and you talk in your class about punctuality, what is involved in punctuality: consideration, not obedience, not saying, 'If you are not there the food will get spoiled'. That is a punishment. Or you say, 'If you are there on time, the food will be better'. That is a reward. You have to go into all that, all the time. That is my point.

So how will you bring about order in a child who is disorderly, as well as in oneself who is disorderly? As a teacher, you know the child's instinct is to obey because he says, 'You know much better than I do. You love me, therefore I'll do what you want me to do'. How will you create a sense of discipline, freedom and order? 'Create': I am using quick words. How will you bring this about? Because freedom is absolutely essential. But is freedom to do what one likes? Bear in mind, sir, Christianity originally said that you cannot do what you want to do; you are doing God's will; you cannot believe anything but what we tell you to believe. It became heresy, torture; all that followed. All this is in the blood of people, is in the background, unconsciously buried inside. Fear. So then order means obedience; and the reaction to that is to do what you want to do, permissiveness, which has spread all over the world.

So how are you going to teach, help the child to understand order, discipline and so on without reward and punishment, without obedience and conformity; and therefore with real freedom? The communists say that this is not possible; human beings are monkeys; we will train them, we will make them conform through fear, through reward. So, if you are a teacher, if you are serious, how will you help to bring about this sense of freedom? Because that is the first thing that is absolutely necessary. At least, I feel so.

Q: When you talk over each problem with the child instead of making him feel he is inferior, one finds the child...

K: That you do. Now, that means that in talking with them you are not putting yourself on a pedestal. You are on their level. You understand what I mean; you are not on their level, of course, because you know something more than they do, but you establish a relationship in which the hierarchical attitude doesn't exist, the teacher up there and the student down here.

Q: This also implies having the same attitude that one has towards the student and learning to be orderly towards one's colleagues and the parents. We are all working together on this problem.

K: Of course, of course, that is what I mean. That is what I said at the beginning. It is *our* school, not your school or my school. Together we are doing this. That brings tremendous vitality. If we are all doing things together, it brings vitality.

Q: I work with pre-school children, 3 years old to 5 or 6. There is a great danger in talking about these things with a 5 year old. He wants to know, and very often he needs to be told what to do.

K: I know, I know. Poor things! Don't torture them. They know nothing about it.

Q: And he is very dependent. I am not putting down what you are saying.

K: Quite right. You are saying the right thing, sir. I know this. Poor things.

Q: So with younger children you must show them, you must live this order in everything you do. You can't go into a class and say, 'We will do mathematics later and now we do our freedom'. That is not a good scheme.

K: Of course, sir.

Q: So in everything you do, you show love for doing the things you are doing. When you are eating, you are eating in order. So it must permeate everything you are doing. I think maybe talking about it must happen as children get older and are more able to assimilate this.

K: Of course, sir, that's right.

Q: I get the feeling now, of what you're saying.

K: There is no established thing at all. If we are going to start a school here we have to start it together, knowing what we want to do, more or less, not completely. There must be a total dedicated togetherness in creating this, otherwise you cannot do it. If we do it without that spirit it will become like any other ordinary school.

(Pause)

To whom are we responsible? To the society? To the parents? To some ideology, however new or dead? To whom are we responsible? Responsibility means, doesn't it, to respond, to respond adequately, to respond adequately to this challenge. The challenge being that it is becoming more and more obvious and necessary that through a different kind of education a new human being comes into being. For that I feel responsible.

Q: So it is not to whom.

K: No. That is just it. I am not responsible to anybody, but I am responsible for the integrity, the seriousness, the thing. I don't even become responsible; I am just that.

Q: Doesn't that integrity and that state of responsibility then include all? To the child obviously we are responsible.

K: Of course, all that. So can we feel responsible for creating a school of this kind?

Q: I feel that even here there are pressures, social pressures and also within ourselves. Pressures that we do inevitably bring, the tendency to want to mould, to shape, to form the child into something else, and to assume that we know what that is.

K: So can we look at all this: ourselves, our pressures, our disorders, our desires to hurt and be hurt? Can we look at it all and say, 'Yes, it is because of that I feel responsible to create a new, different human being'?

Perhaps you will think about it or look at it in a different way: can we together give birth? Because you cannot give birth with one person. (Laughs) Several people are necessary to give birth. Can we give birth to this school in Ojai and be totally responsible?

2

WHAT IS THE RELATIONSHIP OF COOPERATION AND AUTHORITY TO FREEDOM?

Krishnamurti (K): I think we ought to talk over the question of authority, freedom and cooperation. If we are going to form a school at Ojai, and it looks very much as though we're going to have one, and also an educational centre in which the school will be included, we ought to find out how we can build together not only the school but also the educational centre. Is it going to be one man's job or is it going to be a cooperative effort, or is it going to be around an authority which we look up to and therefore accept?

What place has authority in a school of this kind? And what is the relationship of the student to the teacher? And what is cooperation; the cooperation of the parents, the students, the teachers? Is that cooperation based on a formula, a concept, an ideal and therefore authority; or is cooperation something entirely different, not based on authority either of a person or of an idea or an ideology, or the authority of one's own personal image? If there is such authority, can there be cooperation with the parents, with the students, with the teachers? I would like to discuss this, if I may, and I hope you will really discuss this with me.

What is cooperation? We know cooperation is necessary to do anything together. Is it to be based on reward and punishment, or cooperation around an ideology or a person because you believe that person is right or has something and you want to work together with him in order to carry out something which he believes or which he asserts? Then he becomes the authority. All that is implied when one discusses, goes into the question of cooperation and authority and freedom.

In the communist world people get cooperation through punishment and reward. In the capitalist world they get cooperation through reward, money, position, prestige—which doesn't mean that is excluded in the communist world. And in all the religious organisations it is the same principle operating: reward and punishment; and around that there is cooperation, working together.

What is our attitude, our feeling, our action with regard to authority? To me, personally, authority in any form is poison, because I see what is involved in it: domination, favouritism, forming a group around oneself, personal worship, and the feeling that comes with personal authority, a division between the authority and another who has no authority. The word *authority* means, originally, the author, the originator, the one who begins something new. The Church has the authority of Jesus; so-called. In Russia it is Marx and in China Mao Tse Tung. So what is our relationship to authority? I think we ought to be clear on this point before we start a school.

Questioner (Q): Well, if we see that authority breeds fear and dependence and we still see that the thing must get done, then we have nothing to do with authority, with status.

K: Sir, it is terribly difficult. It is much more subtle than merely saying we will have nothing to do with authority. You have experience; you have climbed the mountains and you know how to climb mountains, how to ski or whatever it is, and you become my authority. I don't know, so I work with you. The authority of knowledge, the authority of experience is one thing—the doctor, the scientist, and so on—but if I pose myself as an authority because I know and you don't know, there is authority immediately.

Q: So maybe the question is in what realm there is room for expertise and in what realm there is no place for it.

K: That's it. We are going to find out. Children, as far as I have seen, and also students and grown-ups, like to imitate, they like to conform, they like to adjust themselves to you. They love you; you are friendly to them, and unconsciously you become an authority. But you say, 'All right, I won't exercise authority; I love children'. That is a very dangerous word, because in America the word *love* covers everything: 'I love my country', so I go to war. It covers everything; it is a kind of an umbrella under which you can take shelter for everything. So for the moment let's leave the word *love* out. Sorry, I'm not criticising America, I am just stating it.

How can we bring about a feeling of cooperation? Not, 'I love you but I don't love her, therefore I won't work with her'. Then you form a group; and in a school, if there are groups, it begins to break up. So how do we proceed to understand authority and cooperation?

Q: Couldn't you begin with an open interchange of ideas, without any authoritative quality at all? Simply exchange ideas of what people do know, before you even begin to teach?

K: Will exchange of ideas bring about cooperation? Here we are. We are exchanging ideas. Is that cooperation? What does the word itself mean?

Q: Work together, isn't it?

K: Work together. That is, operate, work, do, create, and so on, all that. Now, does the exchange of ideas bring about cooperation?

Q: No, because I have my ideas and you have your ideas and we battle.

K: Yes, exactly. Opinions, ideas, conclusions. You have your conclusions. They do not bring cooperation. You and I agree about something, as opposed to others who do not agree. I am trying to find out what it means to cooperate, do things together, work together. What is involved in that?

Q: Mustn't you have a common goal to begin with?

Q: But then we're not in relationship. We have a common goal, we are relating to the goal, we are not in relationship.

K: That's right, we are working for the goal, for an object, and therefore if someone is not working with you for that common goal we exclude them. It is much more complex than that and much more subtle. Can we work together if there is no common goal, if there is no authority, if there is no ideology around which we are cooperating, no punishment and reward? Can we do that? Can we work together without punishment and reward, without a common goal, without opinions and judgements? Can we eliminate all that from us?

Q: Krishnaji, could we ask you to go into a little bit more about the lack of common goals? Because we were saying that we are all involved with an educational centre or a school or whatever it is, and that could be defined as a common goal.

K: No, no, leave for the moment the school, the educational centre. I want to find out the nature, the quality, the structure, the substance of cooperation.

Q: Well, you are trying to define something in the positive, so you cannot talk about what cooperation is. When you are cooperating, you're cooperating. So you can talk only about what is not cooperation.

K: I have done that. I said a goal or purpose doesn't bring about cooperation, an ideology does not bring about cooperation, an authority does not bring it, personal worship does not.

Q: Well, that very negation brings about an intensity.

K: That is what I want to find out. When I use the word *negate,* I understand the whole nature of having a goal. It is divisive; it is a thing projected by thought based upon past experience and knowledge. I understand that; therefore I can say I negate that, without any resistance. Without cutting it sharply, I say that it is finished. Now can I say the same thing about ideology? Because for a few months we will agree about that ideology and then suddenly somebody says he does not like that ideology, and we break up. It is the same around a person; that is equally silly, if not more silly than any other. So can I negate all that? Not theoretically, but actually negate it.

From there I ask myself: what is cooperation? Am I in a state of vacuum, or have I negated that which destroys cooperation? I have negated that which is false, which prevents working together. So can I negate this whole sense of "me" who is cooperating with "you"? I like you, therefore I will work with you. I do not like her and therefore I won't work with her. It is really a tremendous question, because we are brought up, educated to cooperate when it is personally, psychologically and financially profitable in different fields. And if it is not profitable then I won't cooperate with you. I will go somewhere else to find cooperation.

Q: Then you are not looking for cooperation.

K: That's it. You really want personal position.

Q: Satisfaction.

K: And that you call cooperation.

Q: Is there any motive for cooperation?

K: We said if there is motive, there is no cooperation. Motive is a goal, reward or punishment, an ideology, a person or a group of persons. So to eliminate all that is to eliminate all motive.

Q: Isn't there a need for cooperation?

K: What do you mean by that word *need*?

Q: Well, I think that if we are going to work together on establishing an educational centre, we are not doing it as individuals.

K: I would not use the word *need* there. We are not discussing the need to cooperate, we are discussing what cooperation is. If I have understood it, I will work with you. You do not have to tell me, I will put my life into it; and in working together we will create it. The need, the money, everything comes from that. First you and I must understand what cooperation is. When that is clear, we do not even ask the need. We say, 'Yes, a school is necessary'.

Q: Are you saying that one isn't being pushed by anything, one just cooperates?

K: What does that mean?

Q: That means that there is no conflict.

K: Yes, sir. Go on. Push more into it.

Q: It means that there is no battle going on between people; there are no subtle competitions, no jealousies, no rivalry.

K: Sir, in a family—father, mother, children—is there cooperation? The father goes off to earn money; the mother looks after the children, cooks, washes and so on. Is that cooperation?

Q: It depends if the mother and the father see clearly the nature of cooperation.

K: But do they? The father goes off to the office. He has his ambitions. He wants competition and all that, and comes home. She has her own particularities—domination, position, all the rest. So there is a subtle battle going on between the husband and wife. The husband is separate and the wife is separate and the children are separate. And yet they all live in the same house. You follow? Is that cooperation?

Q: No, obviously not.

K: Obviously not. Then what that is not, is cooperation. We do not have to define it.

Q: Then in the absence of all those conflicts, those desires, there is cooperation. So there is no definition per se.

K: Through negation you come to the positive. Right?

Q: Yes.

K: Are you like that?

Q: The moment I say that I am cooperative, I am not cooperative.

K: No, have you negated? That is all I mean.

Q: Well, the only real test would be if my mind were absolutely quiet.

K: No, no, I am trying to understand the nature and the structure of cooperation. The nature of it. And I see it is none of these; neither the family nor all that we went through. And

I say: all right, I will wipe it out from myself, because to me cooperation is essential.

Q: You say that you wipe it out, but then it comes back.

K: Ah! Never.

Q: It never comes back.

K: Never.

Q: You see it clearly and then it never comes back.

K: That is right. You never play with a dangerous animal, do you?

Q: I see. And when you see it so absolutely clearly...

K: Then it is out.

Q: Well, when there is that kind of cooperation, it is at a different level.

K: We won't even say *level*. Do we negate first?

Q: Most of us do not, though we say we do.

K: Then it is up to you.

Q: So, you are not talking about cooperation as an ideal outside of ourselves in some state or at some level, but cooperation actually amongst us in the present, that grows and continues to be alive.

K: When that kind of cooperation exists, then we will create together.

Q: And if I'm not mistaken, if this is not here, if we do not have it, I do not believe anything will be created.

K: But wait a minute, sir, look at the difficulty. I may not have negated totally.

Q: Right. Yes.

K: But I'm terribly interested in the school. And as I work with you I begin to discover what I have not negated.

Q: It comes up in the relationship.

K: Of course.

Q: The friction: I don't like you.

K: I wipe it out.

Q: That's what I'm saying. Right.

K: So I begin to learn through the action of working together.

Q: In relationship.

K: Of course, of course, in relationship. So I discover that I have not negated ideals, ideologies in my relationship with you, in doing something together. I say, 'By Jove, I still have that poison in me', and I look at it very carefully—and finished! So it is not that I must first wipe it all out and then cooperate with the building of the school, but in the very act of building, in relationship, about the school, I discover all these things.

Q: Precisely. They come up as you are living.

K: Cooperating for a goal is fairly clear. We have the common goal that we want to build a school, and therefore we say, 'For God's sake don't disturb that goal. Don't disturb any of us. Let's not quarrel. Let's not backbite. Let's not be jealous, because we have common goal'. I don't know if you understand what I am saying.

Q: That is a narrowing process too, isn't it?

K: That is just it. Because we have a common goal we become more and more unintelligent. Because then we say, 'Put aside your personal feelings, for the common goal sacrifice yourself, restrain yourself, hold back'.

Q: So we sacrifice our individual lives...

K: No, don't use the word *individual*. Sir, I am very careful about the usage of words. Therefore let's go slowly.

If we have a common goal, the goal becomes much more important than cooperation. But we have to build a school together. That is not a goal; that is our common interest because we all want to do that. It does not mean I won't discuss it with you. It does not mean I am going to restrain myself from expressing what I feel, but my feeling of cooperation is much stronger than working for a goal. I wonder if I'm making it clear. I think this is fairly clear.

Q: When you talk about goals, it is outside of you and you are not living it.

K: That's right. That is involved too. So in our relationship with each other in bringing about a school, I discover the blockages which prevent cooperation. Because we are concerned only with cooperation now, nothing else. Now, can we so cooperate in building this thing? Then it is our common responsibility: money, looking after the garden, food, clothes, everything. I don't know. I feel that way. That is one thing.

Then let's discuss authority. The word means the originator. It comes from the word *author*, the one who originates, the author of a book, the author of an idea. There is the authority of law, the authority of an ideology, the authority of a personal influence, the authority of experience, the authority of knowledge, and the authority of belief. Christianity believes it has authority from Jesus Christ. That is their final authority, and the Pope is the representative, all the way down to the local priest. There is the authority of an ideology as represented by Marx, Mao Tse Tung, and so on. Now, what place has authority in relationship when we are cooperating together to bring about this school?

Q: It has no place at all.

K: It has no place, but do we understand the full significance of authority?

Q: Well, there's a difference between authority and function. For instance, I might know more than you something spatially about setting up a school. That is not authority. If we are truly cooperating, we can touch on that, we can dip into that and use it.

K: That is, you are separating function from status.

Q: Well, I am trying to discriminate.

K: Yes. What you are saying is right. Look at it. Go slowly, slowly, slowly. Someone says, 'I know how to play the violin'. That is function. But when through function I assume a position, a status, that status becomes the authority, not the function.

Q: And people begin to respond to that.

K: To the status.

Q: Yes.

K: Not to function.

Q: Yes, and it inhibits their own development, their own intelligence.

K: That is right. A cook is looked down upon and a man with money, position, is looked up to.

Q: Why is that?

K: Oh, because he represents what I want to be.

Q: I see. If you want the money, you look up.

K: Yes, I project my image. If a man rides in a Rolls Royce or has position, I want to be that, therefore I respect that, but I do not want to be a cook. So can we always keep to function and never introduce status? Do you understand, sir, how difficult this is? Look at it.

Q: At every moment there is the voice trying to come in and say, 'Look everyone how good a job I'm doing'. It comes in very subtly and it is communicated to everybody, and it starts off this whole process of dependency and fear and everything.

K: Of course, therefore one has to look at it. What is respect? I respect function. If you can do something marvellously, I respect you for it. Right? But we respect not function but status.

Q: But in a practical sense, Krishnaji, when a group of people with different functions, different abilities are all together in one project, the group will tend, fairly logically, to pay attention to the one who knows about carpentry in one area and the one who knows about cooking in this and medical in that. Don't you have to pay attention to the one who has the expertise?

K: I do. I said that I have respect for function.

Q: But it attaches itself to the person who exercises it, not as a person but as a functioning.

K: That is what I am saying. I am respecting function not the person who functions.

Q: If it attaches to the person, the authority immediately comes in.

K: Of course, naturally. See what we are learning from this. That is what I want to get at. We are learning that function and status are two different things, and that when status becomes important, function is disregarded, and therefore status is respected and not function. The excellency of function is to be respected, not status. But now the world respects status, not function. If I have respect for the excellency of function, do I have no respect for the person who has no function?

Q: Or for the person who does his job poorly?

K: Go into it, sir, it is very interesting.

Q: So then I have an image of my...

K: No, what is important? Excellency of function? And not excellency in function? What is important?

Q: Is it perhaps that we think that excellence is something in addition to function?

K: I will make it clear. I respect you because you are excellent in function; you do everything marvellously. And somebody else is not good at function, therefore do I not respect him? So what is important here? I know you are excellent in what you're doing, and I know he is not excellent in what he is doing. So do I respect you and have no respect for this man?

Q: No.

K: Wait, sir, don't say no. See what takes place.

Q: If the man does not function, what is there to respect?

K: Oh, you are only respecting function?

Q: No, but respecting the function is one thing and having a respect for the person is another.

K: Therefore what is important? Respect. Right? For excellency and for the man who cannot do it properly. You respect the man, not the function there. There you respect the function and the man.

Q: Otherwise it is respect with a goal again. You respect *because*, rather than respect.

K: That is it. I have respect, therefore I respect the man and the environment and the animals, and so on; but I have no disrespect for the man who is not good at his job. I respect. I have a feeling of respect. I am concerned with the human being more than with the function. Therefore see what takes place. The human being has created the status. One respects the man who has status, not function, and therefore disrespect for the man who has no status.

Q: If I respect status, I do not respect the man who has status.

K: Yes.

Q: But suppose you have two students and one of the students is performing beautifully and the other one is not because he is lazy. Are you going to respect that?

K: Now, wait a minute. That involves something else. Are you comparing one student against another? The student A is very good in the class and student B is not good. By comparing B with A you are destroying B. No?

Q: Yes, and also A.

K: Of course you are destroying A, but primarily you are destroying B.

Q: But you still have one child who is paying attention and the other one who is not.

K: We go from one thing to the other. Let's stick to one thing at a time. We are talking of authority. Right? Do you accept the authority of excellence, because someone is marvellous at doing something? What is wrong with that acceptance? But if you create that person who is functioning well into an authority, then the mischief begins. Right?

Q: You get a pecking order.

K: A pecking order!

Q: The problem is more in giving the authority and status rather than accepting it.

K: And why do we create authority? Because I am disorderly, confused, and you seem to be orderly, therefore I respect you. I create out of my disorder the authority. See what is happening.

Q: And the responsibility is on you and not on me.

K: Of course. We are learning an awful lot when we are considering authority.

Q: If the student has a desire to achieve a certain function, is there authority?

K: No, say you are teaching me mathematics. You discourage in me the worship of you, don't you? I am a student, and because you are teaching me I get attached to you. This happens all the time. Will you discourage it? Because it is very flattering to you.

Q: Yes, but I think if the student is four years old and...

K: Agreed. There it is necessary. We are coming to something else, sir. Presently we will come to it.

So to understand this question of authority in relationship one has to be extraordinarily aware of oneself. In relationship in a school, we are a whole community by ourselves, and therefore we have to be extraordinarily alert to see that we are not creating status, we are not creating disrespect for human beings, but have respect only for function, and do not make ourselves into an authority for a student. All this requires great watchfulness, awareness of oneself.

So what is freedom then? We said cooperation can only exist if there is no goal, if there is no punishment and reward, if there is no ideology. An ideology becomes the authority. Then also we asked what authority is. A disorderly community makes a politician into the authority; because they are disorderly, the politician is disorderly. If I were orderly, I would not elect any of these birds, because they are totally disorderly. But authority in function is obviously necessary. You know much more about carpentry than I do, but when out of that function you create a status, the status becomes the authority, not function, and therefore you function inefficiently because you want to keep your status. And there is authority when there is no clarity. A community which is disorderly creates its own disordered leader. Mussolini, Hitler, Stalin are all examples. It is clear. Now, what is the relationship of cooperation, authority, to freedom?

Q: It seems that where there is authority there can be no freedom.

K: Right. So which are you going to bring about? Freedom? And therefore no authority? No authority in the deep sense of that word. But when you say no authority, then people say, 'All right, I am as good as you. I won't accept that you are a better carpenter, I am as good a carpenter as you'. That is too silly. What is the relationship of all this to freedom? Can freedom exist where there is authority? Can freedom exist where there is no cooperation? Obviously not. So the three go together, don't they? Of course. They are not separate things, they all are interrelated.

Can we create such a school? It would be the most marvellous thing in the world because there never existed such a school. (Pause) If we did it, it would be something original, creative, and we would create different human beings.

Q: What do you say to the man who says there is no freedom in authority, when the kids want to come in and they want to take their bread crumbs and sprinkle them on the floor?

K: (Laughs) I would talk to them. At what age can you talk to these children intelligently?

Q: Around 6 and 7.

Q: No. No way.

Q: Yes you can if you talk to them in a...

K: To some of them you can, to some you cannot. So go on, explore it. You will see, you will come to something yourself. What we are concerned with demands that there should be a communication verbally as well as non-verbally with the student, doesn't it? Can you communicate all this to the boy or girl of 6?

Q: I highly doubt it unless that child is extremely mature, and I've never seen that.

K: No. Don't force the child to be mature, for God's sake.

Q: Because he will interpret that as moralising.

K: Yes, moralising or whatever it is. So at what age can you discuss, talk these things over?

Q: Only at the very end, if it all.

K: So what will you do?

Q: I think it is important to relate to each child as a unique entity. Some children, you can tell.

Q: The kids get into a fight and smack each other around.

K: I am asking a different question. How can you prevent a child from smacking another child? Not after the incident. You are dealing with after the incident; I want to prevent it. Now, how will you do it? That is one problem. Wait, we will come back to that. If you are going to have children from age 6 to age 12, and you can only talk, discuss, explain, go into things at the age of 12, you will have very few, won't you? Go on, sir, explore it. I don't want to explore it for you. I have done it.

Q: Explain it to the child. Sit down and talk to these children.

K: Some of them you can talk to, others you may not be able to.

Q: But even little children watch television, they watch Sesame Street and so on. Why couldn't you explain it in a way that they understand?

K: We will do that, but to go into a little more difficult things, as we have been discussing. To prevent smacking not after the incident but before the incident is much more important.

Q: Well, one of the reasons a child will smack is because he feels that he is not cared for.

K: Of course.

Q: So it goes without saying that you will try to create an atmosphere in which each child feels very deeply that he is cared for, that what he says, what he feels is respected, is gone into.

Q: Can you help the children come to terms with their own violence by expressing what is going on in them? Can you show a child his own disorder, or something like that?

K: Sir, look at it. He lives in a world of violence: cinemas, photographs, newspapers; his own books he reads are full of violence. He is surrounded by violence, and you are telling him not to be violent.

Q: Well, doesn't it really depend on the teacher?

K: We are finding out, exploring what to do. The child is surrounded by violence. His whole environment is violent, and he comes to the school already conditioned to violence.

Q: We have to make it clear who we are talking about. Are we talking about kids 5 to 10 or are we talking about kids from 10 on through adolescence? I think it is different.

K: Yes. So what is the school going to be? From 6 to 14 or only 6 to 12?

Q: We really haven't decided.

K: I don't want my child who has been with you for four years or six years suddenly thrown into the world, and you saying, 'Go to a local high school'.

3

A SCHOOL OF THIS KIND IS NECESSARY BECAUSE THE WORLD IS IN CHAOS

Krishnamurti (K): A school of this kind is necessary because the world is in chaos, and any serious parent who feels really responsible could not and will not, if he loves his children, allow them to go to ordinary schools where they will be cannon fodder, business fodder or scientific fodder. From what one has heard and read and observed, children right throughout the world are in real trouble. I am not talking of neurotic children, but ordinary children; they are really at a loss. There are those whose parents are divorced or separated; that is a great shock to them. They do not feel secure, and from that insecurity all the violence and brutality is taking place.

We will start a school here in Ojai. Can we give a sense of feeling and atmosphere in which the children have no trouble whatsoever; where they do not feel troubled, but protected, secure, feeling completely at home, where they are really cared for physically, mentally, their clothes, their behaviour, everything, so that they have security, freedom and a sense of feeling that they live in a world where there is no trouble for them, where they have no problems which must be solved? We will discuss what that means. As you know, I have talked to a lot of children in India and here and in Europe. They are really at a loss. You must have noticed. They are very troubled. I saw the face of a boy the other day. He was young, I should think about 8 or 9, he looked so worried, so unhappy, you know, his face showed everything.

Can we in our schools have total security so that the child feels really secure, physically, protected? In a certain way, children do not like to be protected. They say, 'We will run away from you'. But I am using the word *protection* in the sense of caring, not imposing authoritarian assertions. And freedom. Freedom and authority do not go together, but they need a certain enclosure. So, freedom with a sense of real, deep psychological protection. Because, if I may, when I was with Dr Besant, they have looked after that side. They gave tremendous protection. Not the absurd protection of attachment, domination, guidance and being told what to do, what not to do: 'You are a liar, you must not, you must be this, that', which some consider to be protection, and at the end of it the child says, 'I don't want to talk to my parents'. They have had enough, and the say 'I don't want even to see them', and gradually a feeling of great inward trouble is built in them.

Can we together create such an atmosphere, such an actual feeling of complete security? Then the question of freedom becomes trust. If I trust you I am free. If I do not trust you, I am not free. Even *trust* is the wrong word. Can we establish between the student and the teacher a feeling of real affection in which is implied trust, companionship, caring? Do we agree to this: security, freedom—not guidance but yet they need guidance; not discipline and yet they need order? We cannot give them problems to solve, emotional problems, psychological problems. They will have problems later on, but while they are the age of 10, 12, 15, why should they have problems? I think problems exist because the parents are ugly parents. The children hear the quarrels, the nagging, all that goes on, and they do not want to grow up like that; and yet by circumstances or by society they are forced to become like that. So can we provide an education in which the children have no psychological trouble, or even physical trouble? And can we provide a sense of great security for them, and a feeling of freedom which can only come into being when they really trust you, are not afraid of you? Can we create such a thing?

If we agree to that, then the next difficulty that arises is that they come to the school already conditioned. They come already conditioned, either with a rich man's conditioning or middle-class conditioning or very poor conditioning. They come conditioned religiously, politically, economically and, especially in England, class conditioning, which is known through language, the right way to pronounce, the right words, the right voice. The children come conditioned. Can we help them to uncondition and not fall into another conditioning? And can that be done through teaching any subject?

Say, for example, I am a mathematics teacher. I would like to teach them order, because mathematics is complete order. I would like to convey to them this order and help them to understand order because they come out of a world of disorder and are conditioned by that disorder, and therefore they react according to that conditioning, saying, 'Here is a place where I can do what I like, I can shout, I can do anything'. So in teaching mathematics my concern would be first to bring order in their life. I won't tell them what it means, order in their life. They won't even know what it means. So how am I, in teaching mathematics, which is order, to convey to them the necessity of complete inward order? It becomes very exciting for me as a mathematician. It is something new. I go along discovering. So, in a class of five, ten, fifteen, I would talk not about mathematics but order and what it means.

Q: One could do this with all subjects.

K: Yes, with all subjects. I would explain to them that I am in disorder as well as they are, that I am not on top of disorder. So we are both concerned. We are both learning. That puts me in a right relationship with the child. I am not superior; I am in disorder, which is true. I, the teacher, I am in disorder, I quarrel, I get angry, I smoke, I drink, and so on. By talking to you, both of us are going to learn what order is, so we both are together. That brings a new quality. Then he feels free to say, 'Look, sir, what do you mean?' So can this be done in every subject, through every subject? It opens a lot of doors, doesn't it? History and science.

Q: It also breaks down the divisions between subjects.

K: That is right, and the sense of competition which is ingrained by the conditioning. The father comes home full of aggressive competitiveness, and tells his wife, 'Look, I got a better job. I'm better than him'. And the child absorbs it. And in the class he is compared with somebody who is better than he is, and so on. Can we not have grades, all that business, and wipe away the feeling of competitive learning, the competitive drive which ultimately ends up in hate, in jealousy and ruthlessness? All that is involved in it. Can we create such a school? If we cannot it is not worth doing it. Right?

Q: But I think we can, sir.

K: I think we can, otherwise we wouldn't talk about it. If we cannot do it it's not worth doing it. As we want to do it, we can do it. We will find methods, systems, we will create our own teachers, our own ways of making the child do things with his hands.

Q: Krishnaji, may I raise what might be a question in the minds of some people who do not know about your teaching and the implications of it? For instance, you said earlier in this discussion that the world is in chaos and that it is a very violent, ugly world. Now, many people will say you are possibly presenting a picture of the school where a child is overprotected and he will come out into this dreadful world totally unable to cope.

K: Yes, I know. That is the eternal question in the schools in India and at Brockwood. I think the real answer to that is: if our education creates, cultivates that intelligence in the students then they will meet the chaos in the world. They must meet the chaos in the world, they cannot withdraw from it. It is our job as teachers to bring about that intelligence. And that intelligence comes when there is complete security, no trouble for the child. No trouble in the sense of no worries, no problems of whether I should go with my mother or with my father, whether I am deserted, lonely—all those ugly things at age 13, and the overemphasis on sex, all that. Intelligence comes out of that freedom and the sense of giving a feeling that the child is to enjoy life, to look at flowers, to look at the birds, to feel things. That intelligence will meet this rotten thing called civilisation. It is our job. Otherwise what is the point of having a school? What is the point of giving one's life to a lot of children who will be just like other children?

If I had a son or a daughter, that would be my concern. I don't want them to go to an ordinary school or to an 'advanced' school or to a school where they are taught through audio-visual machines. I want them to be human beings meeting human beings, not machines. If I were a parent I would consider all this. And if there was a school not of that kind, I would give up buying a Cadillac or a Lincoln or something, because it is my duty to have responsibility for these children. But, unfortunately I want the Cadillac, the trips to Europe and then the education if I can do it; (Laughs) my pleasures first and my children afterwards. We are saying your children first and your ugly pleasures later.

Q: Sir, I think there are parents in this country who are concerned.

K: I personally think the field is ripe, it is there for the asking. As you know, we have started other schools in America, but they all failed because of people who are really uneducated getting into this field. But if our intention, our real serious purpose is to give this thing, the *foyer*, the ambience, the environment, the house where it can grow, oh, we can do so much. My Lord!

Q: Sir, doesn't this mean we have to start with young children?

K: Yes, of course, young children up to the age of, I don't know, 12 or 15.

Q: That is why it is important to get the parents.

K: The parents, not just the children. Quite right. So whoever is going to be responsible for the school, a director and an assistant director, both of them have to see the parents, both of them have to find the right kind of children; children who are not drugged, not already sexual, all that.

I don't know if you have noticed, passing schools, how coarse, how old and destroyed the children are. It is peculiar that when they get to puberty their whole look changes and they lose that quality of innocence, you know, that quality of brightness and sharpness and asking clear, direct questions. Can we prevent that loss? I think right education does prevent that.

I would have an assembly every morning of all the teachers, the parents, the children, the gardener, everybody, and I would talk to them about observation. Not concentration but observation. When they came into the room, I would say, 'Sit down and look. Look out of the window. See the trees, see the light, see the moving leaves, the birds. And look, absorb everything. After doing that, then watch yourself, observe yourself'. We would do that for five minutes then somebody could get up and read something or sing something. Begin the day with the feeling that you have taken the world inside you. We can create extraordinary human beings all right.

When they come to the book, there too I say, 'Before you pick up the book, look about you. Look out of the window so that you have had enough looking out the window, so that you won't look out of the window. Look at it. Look at everything you want to see. Soak your eyes with it. Then when you pick up the book, you have finished looking out'. Then they don't say, 'I must concentrate', and have conflict between wanting to look and the beastly book. (Laughs)

If I were a teacher, I would let the students flower. If they are angry, I would let them be angry. Let anger flower, but not into action. That is, if I am angry, let it flower in me, and in the flowering I watch the flowering. I don't deny it, I don't cut it off, I don't say, 'It is ugly. It is beautiful. It is rational. It should be, shouldn't be'. I let it flower. As I observe the flowering of it, it dies away. I would like to tell that to the children so that their mind, their body, their feelings are all sensitive, alive.

Let's see if we are clear. We want a place where children come, where they feel completely at home and completely secure. So, they have complete security and it is our business as teachers to see that they have it. What is implied in all that, we can discuss. And you give them the feeling that they can trust you—about their ugliness, their sex, their anger, their anything. They can trust you, and that brings a feeling of great freedom in their relationship. Then we see that they have no troubles, which the parents, which the cinema, which the other children foist on them. Here you give them a feeling that they are here to be children, to learn, not to have to solve your terrible problems. And you make them feel at home, because their own home is not a home any more. If we do this, in teaching, say, mathematics, convey how to observe, look, all that, then out of that comes the incredible intelligence which will face the world which they have to live in. And they will face it with delight, because then it becomes a challenge to meet it and not to escape from it.

Q: Do you want to go into the educational centre today or another day?

K: Oh yes, we can go on with the educational centre. Sir, you know what the educational centre is? We are trying to get land. On part of that land we want a school, but also a place where serious people can gather. Serious means good people who come together to discuss these teachings and how to let these teachings operate in their daily life. That is one thing for the educational centre, because that means educating the older people. As you are educating the younger people, we are educating each other at the educational centre. That means a place where people can come. They may remain outside in the motels and all that, but a few of them can stay with us as guests, and for two or three weeks sit together. Not be entertained, not learn from you or from me or from somebody else how to be sensitive, but in talking over, in discussing, in examining, exploring, penetrating they will become sensitive, and so on. There will be a library; there will be tapes; there will be an assembly hall. It is a place of great studiousness, in the sense you are there not only to enjoy yourself, but you are really concerned about changing yourself, bringing a different way of living, and so on. There will be a place for a bigger gathering, in the assembly hall. There will be children—I think it is important for the children to listen to what the older people are discussing, with a sense that they take part in it. The children are not kept out of it, but they come into this so that they take part in what is happening, see how older people look at life, how they talk, how confused they are, how bitter, how angry, how hateful. They get the feeling of it so they begin to understand. It is an educational centre in that sense: total education, physical, psychological and all that. My word!

4

A NEW CULTURE COMES ONLY WITH RELIGION

Krishnamurti (K): If I were a parent, would I like my son or daughter to go to a residential school for four months and not see them again for four months, when they are just at the age when they are fun to talk to? If I am a serious parent, that is the age I would like to keep them at home to play with, to talk with, have companionship and so on. So what age would you consider them old enough not to be conditioned too much, not to be too attached to the family?

Questioner (Q): If we didn't take 6 and 7 year olds it seems to me then parents would probably feel they had to put their children in an ordinary public school, which would be unfortunate, I think.

Q: Wouldn't it be possible to have enough children from the community and children of teachers to start them at the first grade 6 year old age, and then let older children, perhaps from 11 to 14, be residential students? It seems a pity to miss the chance of having the young ones.

K: Sir, start from the other end. What kind of school is it to be? You know what *school* means? In Latin it means leisure, and it means a place of academy, where there is discussion. Start from that end rather than what kind of children. We will come to that. What is it we want? Bearing in mind the idea of leisure—not to amuse yourself, but to have leisure to look, to think, to reason, to observe. You must have leisure. If you look at it from that point of view, if that is the framework, what would you have? There is the educational centre on one side, where leisure is essential; otherwise people cannot discuss; they will say, 'I have to go immediately to my office'. You must have leisure, a period of time where you can sit and discuss, go into things, get to know them, all that. That demands leisure. Now, in relation to that, the school is also a kind of leisure. At what age would you begin? Forget the local people, forget everything else and ask what ages you would have.

Q: I think children between the ages of 8 and 10 are free enough of their parents that they can be without their mother and not have to be constantly supervised.

K: Yes, if we begin at 8, and a few at 6, and up to what age?

What would be your experience, sir? You have observed various schools in California, what would you say would be the best age to begin, knowing what we want, knowing all our background?

Q: From the point of view of a child, the earliest possible time when they can have the kind of exposure we are talking about, the better it is for the child. I think the conditioning is very important, don't you, Krishnaji?

K: Yes, I do. Suppose I hear of a school of this kind. I would come as a parent to talk with all of you, and I want to see what kind of human beings you are. Not your ideas, but what you have, how I feel towards you and you feel towards me. I would like to look at you to see whether you are really nice people, whether you say one thing and do something else, and so on. I want to have some contact with you. So I would spend a few days with you or a week with you. And then I would make up my mind, knowing what is involved: money; knowing I have to be here in the valley or Ventura to earn a livelihood and that my children would be here, and I want to be near them sometimes, and so on. So when they are 6 or 8, you have to interview the parents. Now, who is going to undertake to do that? Who will be responsible? Who will be responsible to meet the parents, take time and trouble to show them what kind of people we are? Who will make it his responsibility to say this has to be done?

Q: The director and staff are the people to do it.

K: Yes.

Sirs, what kind of school are we going to have? That is much more important than the building and the land. What kind of thing are you going to create? You see, I would never call it a K school. It sounds sectarian. That's one superficial, rather tawdry reason. If we have the place, what kind of thing are you going to create out of it? Because you will be responsible. I am gone. Not that I am necessary, but I am gone. I won't be back until next year. And I think it matters tremendously how the school begins.

Q: Sir, if I may think aloud. I think some of the statements that were made initiated the thrust of the school—having concerned parents and an atmosphere of trust and affection;

being a place where adults and children will grow together, where the curriculum and so on, all of these things, are dealt with in a totally different way.

K: Yes, that I understand. But I am talking about the soil, the ground in which the thing grows. If you haven't the soil, it won't grow. So what kind of soil are we going to prepare? You may start in December, let us say. You have now eight months, and you have soil where you are going to dig, cultivate. By soil I mean not the actual soil, but religious soil in the sense that we are talking about. Or is it a soil which will produce a different human being merely socially, unrelated to the soil? Is it going to be a religious soil, which I think it should be, otherwise you cannot create a new culture. Historically, from what little I have read and the little I have talked about with historians, a new culture comes only with religion, because it is a new seed, new *élan*, new energy, new burst, a new flame. Are we prepared to create that soil? I am asking what kind of soil you are going to prepare. I think that is very important. You will get all the sanctions, all the legal stuff, all that, but will all of you prepare the soil? As a director are you prepared for this? I'm sorry to put it bluntly.

Q: I understand.

K: You will have the help of the Foundation; they are behind this. Who will be responsible for this show? Will you have that "religious", in quotes, feeling so as to create something which will burst? Not just, 'We will try. We will do this. We will...'

You see, unfortunately my job is to go out and talk. If I were here, I know how I would do it. I know what I would do. If it became my dharma, my duty or whatever it is, I would say, 'I know how to create it', because I would be bursting with it. And because of this, everything will come right: money, land, sanctions, everything. Because the thing is like a fountain that has to erupt. It will erupt somewhere. Can you do this? Can all of you do this? We are starting something which must endure for several hundreds of years—like Nalanda University. They were essentially religious in the deep sense, but they went off. But can we here do it? Can all of you do it? I think that's much more important to discuss than how to get the outward structure or the permissions and so on. So can we create this thing together?

(Pause)

I will tell you, sirs, what is essential in this. I understand certain things now. We have to meet very often, have leisure to talk about all this. You plant a seed; it has to have leisure, darkness, light, rain, sunshine. Can this be done? That means, can we have leisure to sit down and talk about all this till we are soaked up to our gills?

Here we are, we want to start the school, and we want to start it from the very beginning on a right basis. We cannot plant an oak and expect a palm tree. So it must be right from the very beginning. How can we arrange that we all meet, discuss, have leisure to look, feel, create? This is important. The school is important. So we can dig, we can dig into the soil.

Children will come to you, a boy or a girl from 6 or 8 to whatever it is. Living in this country, they are already exposed to the cinema, violence, the newspapers, the magazines, the comics; the little boys already wanting excitement, guns. I was walking once in Hollywood and there were two boys on either side of the road. And a bullet went by quite close. I looked round and these two boys had guns, real guns, and they were laughing at me. Little boys! I laughed, we joked and

J. KRISHNAMURTI

I passed on. So take all that into account. They come already with tremendous excitement in life, wanting excitement. So they come conditioned even at 6 or 8. In this country it is becoming appalling. In India it takes a different form. There it is docile obedience: 'Do not lift your head till you're talked to'. It is terrible there. Here it is the opposite. They come with that. How will you unwind them? How will you make them feel? Even at 8, let them have fun, but not that kind of fun. That is no fun at all. How will you unwind them? How will you uncondition them? There you are. Discuss this, sir.

Q: What would be the relationship between the school and the outer world? I mean, is the school going to be an enclosed garden? What will the interchange be?

K: I would have an enclosed garden for a while, and then you can let them out.

Q: If you have this protected, safe environment, really protected, then later on anything can happen to them. We saw this in Rishi Valley.

K: Quite right, sir.

Q: But children who started with us and went straight through never forgot and they were totally different.

K: That is what the Jesuits did. They took boys and girls at the age of 7. They said, 'Give me a boy of 7 and he will never be other than a Jesuit'. That is one form of conditioning, but I am asking: how you will uncondition them, unwind them? How will you give them a different kind of fun?

Q: Sir, with this collection of people, parents and teachers, the whole reason for their being there is this seriousness, this religious feeling. It has not been done.

K: It has not been done.

Q: It wasn't done at Rishi Valley. I don't know what is going on at Brockwood, but in Rishi Valley we didn't do it. I don't know of anywhere else that has really done it.

K: Forget those places. Now can we?

Q: If we really do it, sir, then all these other things...

K: ...will follow. Now how do we do it, sir? You see, in ancient India, from what I have been told, there was the guru. Not in the cheap sense. He was married, he had children and he had other children brought to him, and they lived with him. They did everything together. He was a religious man. He was a moral man. He did puja, whatever they did in the old days. I mean, he was a very disciplined man in the old sense; and to him religious life was the only life. He set—if I may use the word—an example, but the example did not crush the student. At least I am interpreting it that way. Generally examples destroy children. Is it going to be that kind of school where all of us bring our children and we live with them, they live with us?

In Los Angeles or one of those big cities I believe they are experimenting. I read it some time ago or somebody told me. A whole group of people bought a block of flats. They had about thirty families with their children, and they knocked down certain walls so that the children could go from room to room, enter into any room, run about all over the block. For one week one family looked after the laundry, the cooking, the shopping and all that. The next week another family did it. I was told the children were extraordinary, because they met everybody. The old people sat with them and joked with them, told them stories, and when they got bored they left to run off to some thing else. But it was not a religious thing—they drank, they smoked. But they said it was really quite extraordinary to see the children's faces.

Now, can we create this thing together? Have a religious soil, and therefore it would be tremendously rich soil, not poor soil. Being very rich it can take anything. Can we do this? We are not totally religious, but we will be totally religious. If you are given a group of children, how will you make them religious? Not *make them*—I am using a quick phrase—it is not make them in the sense of giving example, conditioning, all that. How will you bring to them or make them feel the religious way of life?

You see, that is what I would like, if we get this property, that when I enter it, I feel, 'My God, this is a sacred place'. Because it is sacred I won't smoke, I can't drink, I can't be vulgar. The very feeling exists there. That feeling makes me behave, not forces me but because it is right to behave that way. I smell it. (Laughs) Can this be done here by all of us?

Q: I see that to have this religious spirit, that is the seed, that is what generates and produces all the rest of it.

K: Of course. Absolutely. You have to have a good, rich brain. And one has to be terribly sensitive, not to one's own demands, but sensitive. And you have to have the sense of meditation and all that is involved in this. It is the educational centre and the school that will give the necessary soil. Gosh, I feel I would love to give all that and stay here, but I cannot, I must not. We will do it, sirs. Now let's proceed.

(Pause)

You know, sirs, it is said that the Benedictine monks held the light in the Dark Ages of Europe. The 14th to 16th Century was the Renaissance. Before that were the Dark Ages, and they held the light of knowledge. They were supposed to be the people who were enlightened. All around them was darkness. We have to be that. Because the world is mad.

One has to be completely dedicated to this. Sorry to put it that way. Nothing else matters but this. It is like having a baby: the mother gets up at two, three, four o'clock; whether she is asleep or awake, it is the baby first. I did that with Radha [Daughter of the Rajagopals], changed the diapers I don't know how often. Complete dedication. The mother is dedicated. She is not even dedicated; the baby is *there*. She does not say, 'I am dedicated'. One must have the capacity, the drive—capacity in the sense of creating from nothing. Dedication implies capacity, and it implies also learning, quickly learning. Capacity for learning and the capacity to bring about a co-operative spirit to make one feel that we must work together. That is an extraordinary thing to have. And care, affection and love, all this is involved in it. That is real dedication. If we have it, the place will burst with laughter.

5

ONLY WHEN THERE IS NO AUTHORITY WILL YOU LEARN ABOUT YOURSELF

Krishnamurti (K): I believe we are going to talk over together this morning the question of education. We are going to have a school here and I am sure serious people are interested in this question. This is not a talk by me; we are going to have a dialogue about it rather than have a discussion. The word *discussion* means, I think, argument, through argument to find what is right opinion. Whereas a dialogue is a conversation between two friends about something they are both interested in seriously. So this is a dialogue rather than a verbal, intellectual, argumentative exchange.

I wonder why we are educated at all, if we are, why we go to schools, colleges and universities. What does it mean to be educated? Why should one be educated? Is it to conform to the pattern of existing society, acquiring enough knowledge to act skilfully in that society to have a livelihood? Does to be educated mean adjusting oneself to society and follow all the dictates of that society? This has become a very serious problem right throughout the world, I am quite sure. The ancients, both in Egypt and in India, and China of course, thought of education not in terms of society, nor in terms of merely conforming to the edicts of society; they were concerned with the culture of the mind, with the culture of a mind that is capable of intelligent action in society, not merely conforming to the pattern of society. Leaving the ancients aside, one looks around the world at the awful mess that is going on, the butchery in China, the threatening wars, the tyranny, the lack of freedom and so on. And in every country there are highly educated people, highly technological, skilled in their action, yet what has education brought about? What has education, in the orthodox sense of that word, made man into? So, we ought to have a dialogue about this.

Is education merely to cultivate one segment of the mind, one part of the brain as memory, acquiring knowledge and using that knowledge skilfully? That is what most of us are educated for; we are conditioned for that. The rest of the psychological, wider entity of people is totally disregarded. Is it possible to "educate"—we use the word *educate* in quotation marks—is it possible to educate the whole of man, including his brain, intellectually, that is, to have the capacity to think clearly, objectively, and act efficiently, non-personally, and also to enter into a field which is generally called spiritual? Again, that is a rather doubtful word. Is this possible to do in a school, college and university, that is, to educate the totality of man instead of cultivating memory, as we do, and depending on that memory to act skilfully in our labours? That cultivation of memory and dependence on that is part of the degeneration of humanity, because then man becomes merely mechanical, always acting in the field of the known— the known being the accumulated experiences, the great deal of words put into books, the collection of centuries of knowledge, and always acting within that field. Is that not a degenerating factor in our human life? Because when you are acting in the field of the known all the time, which is in the field of knowledge, knowledge becomes traditional and you are then acting according to a past pattern set by various scientists, philosophers, psychologists, and the theologians with their persuasive methods. So then the brain must be very conditioned, it has no flexibility, and so gradually, as is happening in the world, there is degeneration in art, in literature, and in our relationship with each other. That degeneration must end up in war, in hatred, in antagonism. If you consider it impersonally, not as Americans and Europeans and so on, but as human beings confronted with this problem, that is actually what is happening. One can see the destructive nature of always operating with, or in, the field of knowledge; our schools, colleges and universities condition our minds to that. Seeing the fact of that, what can we do?

Questioner (Q): Can you give us some examples of degeneration in this culture?

K: I do not think examples are going to help. You can see it, sir; politicians are corrupt.

Q: But there has always been corruption.

K: Is that an excuse?

Q: But look, degeneration implies that things are getting worse and worse.

K: No, the meaning of that word *degeneration* is not being at the highest point of excellence, not having the highest excellence in thought, in ourselves not in somebody else. Not having that highest excellence in morality in our relationship points, surely, to degeneracy. It is not that at other times and other historical periods there has not been degeneracy; civilisations go down, are destroyed because they become degenerate. We are asking if our education throughout the world is giving us, helping us to bring about that excellency in ourselves, in our morality, in our thinking, in our reactions, in all the structure of human existence.

Q: Do you think you can teach anybody to attain that state if they don't want it?

K: Why don't you want it?

Q: Even if we do want it, we come here year after year to hear the talks, but we don't learn.

K: You want it. Then what do you do about it? We want a kind of education that is concerned with the whole person, the whole of man, not just the cultivation of a certain segment of man but the totality of man. There is no such education; no university, no school, no college offers that. And of course religions aren't concerned with that; they are concerned with dogma, with belief, with rituals and authority. So what shall we do?

Q: Could you give an example of actual immorality?

K: Oh, my Lord! I can't. (Laughs) Do you think it is right to kill somebody for your country? Do you think that is right? Oh, you know; I do not have to give examples!

Q: Why not?

K: Because it is dangerous to give examples.

Q: Mr Krishnamurti, you asked what we can do. One thing we can do is to question within, we can question the authority of these teachers, we can question why we are doing what we are doing, we can question how we are conditioned by all of these things. We can find out for ourselves through ourselves in relationship by asking questions. That is how we can do it.

K: Not only that, sir. If you had a son or a daughter and were deeply concerned, as you must be concerned, what would you do?

Q: In talking about structured education about trying to find how to be free, I don't understand how that can be done without taking recourse to a methodology.

K: You want a method.

Q: I do not want a method, I want to understand how it can be done without one.

K: We are going to find out, sir. First look at the problem before we ask what to do. Look at the problem all round. I think if we can look into the problem without the question of what to do, then the problem itself will answer, we will find the way out of it, but not without looking at the problem all round, being totally involved with the problem, totally committed to that problem. You have that problem, it isn't that you must be committed to it, it is your problem. If you are a parent it would be tremendous agony to find out what to do. And what to do can only come about if we understand the problem itself, the depth of the problem, the seriousness, the complexity of the problem. Without looking at that, we say give us a method, but the method is part of this deterioration.

Q: Seeing the complexity of the problem takes time, and children are growing, they haven't got time.

K: Yes, sir, children are growing but we have an hour here. (Laughs) We can, during that hour go into this question to see the depth of this question.

Q: I experience the problem as a dichotomy. I experience a division when I am guiding students, trying to lead them towards searching themselves when I need to disseminate knowledge. To achieve the confluence of those two is what I am searching for. How does one do that?

K: The dichotomy is the division between using knowledge and being free from knowledge. The meaning of the word *art* is to put everything in life in its right place. Please understand the meaning of that word first—to put everything that is concerned with living in its right place. That is the meaning of that extraordinary, beautiful word *art*. Learn the place of knowledge and learn the freedom from that, then there is no dichotomy, there is no division.

Please, I would like to go back to education. Doesn't education mean to learn? The word *school* means a place where you are learning. Now, here is a school, and we are learning. I am learning and you are learning. We are trying to learn or trying to find out the depth of that word *education*. We are trying to find out whether man can be free totally and yet live with the knowledge which we have acquired, which doesn't condition us, which doesn't shape our minds and our hearts.

As one observes in the world, wherever one goes, knowledge has become the factor of conditioning the mind to a certain pattern according to which you act. If I am a communist, that pattern of thinking and acting brings about certain misery and so on. This is happening right through the world and this is what we call education, whether it is education under Mao or education under the politburo or under the capitalist society, or other societies. Where there is the cultivation of a particular segment of human life disregarding the rest, it must inevitably bring about human degeneration. That is obvious. So we are asking if it is possible to educate human beings, from childhood and beyond, to cultivate, to nurture the whole outward and inward totality of man. That is, for me, right education. Is it possible in our life to educate ourselves completely, totally, inwardly as well as outwardly?

Q: You are saying that to break out of the limitations and find new things about education and do new things like create peace in the world and in ourselves, and create love in the world and in ourselves, we have to set up research programmes to do that.

K: Sir, let us put it this way. You have a son and a daughter. What are you going to do with those children, how are you going to educate them? What is your responsibility? Have you any responsibility? If you have responsibility, which means care, attention, love, what are you going to do with those children?

Q: Sir, we're talking about schools and education. It seems to me that any school, whether it be a Krishnamurti school or any school no matter how ideologically instituted, becomes an authority and conditions.

K: Yes, we are going to go into that question of authority and conditioning, but you are not ready.

Q: Sir, I have a daughter. One thing I have noticed is that I am conditioned, and I am conditioning her through my conditioning. I have to be aware of mine. I see that. It seems to me I have to help her understand the rest of conditioning, of the whole society around her that she is growing up in.

K: Are you saying, sir, that in a school, both the educator and the educated are conditioned?

Q: Yes.

K: I have been at this game for fifty years, sir! (Laughter) I have helped to form several schools in India. One of the major problems has been how to deal with the parent who is conditioned and the children also conditioned because they live with their parents, with the society, with their group; and the teacher is also conditioned. They are conditioned in the sense that they are prejudiced, they are violent, they are nationalistic, class conscious—the rich and the poor, the Hindu, the Muslim, the Christian. Now, how to deal with this problem, both at home and in the school, is the question we are discussing now.

You are a teacher, I am the student, the child. You are aware that you are conditioned, and I, the student, am not aware of it because I am still too young. I am being conditioned by television, by magazines, by my friends and so on. Now, how will you deal with this? Just first look at it. How will you deal with this problem? You are conditioned and the student is conditioned; your child is conditioned and the teacher, the educator is conditioned. We have tried this, that is why I am talking about it. In the school the teacher and the student are both conditioned. For the teacher to wait till he is unconditioned he might just as well wait the rest of his life. So the question is whether he and the student in their relationship in a school can uncondition themselves. That is, in teaching or before giving certain facts about mathematics and so on, discuss this problem, talk it over with the students. Say, 'I am conditioned, and you are conditioned', and explain all the complexities of conditioning, the result of that conditioning. Show them the picture, the real picture, not your fanciful, imaginative picture, but the actual picture of a human being's conditioning, as a Jew, as a Muslim, as this or that, and how they are at each other's heads. I would discuss this problem and have a dialogue, go into this with the students, every day, as part of the school work. Then the teacher begins to uncondition himself and the student at the same time.

Q: But there is no method?

K: Of course. How can there be a method? The method is our conditioning. You follow, sir?

Q: Yes, absolutely.

K: Therefore it becomes very alive, intelligent, active, creative.

Q: At the moment that it is happening.

K: So the teacher and the student have to establish a relationship. That means a relationship not of one who knows and the other who does not know. The establishment of right relationship between the teacher and the student is imperative. And the teacher has the responsibility, he is dedicated to this. The father is not, because he has to go to the office, he hasn't time, and the mother hasn't time either. So the teacher, the educator becomes tremendously important. It is the highest profession in society, not the lowest, as it is now. You and I see this. Now what are we going to do about it?

Q: Krishnamurti, you just said the mother and father have no time because they have to work all day; the father has to go to the office. That is a big problem, and I don't want you to skip over it because that is disturbing a lot of people who have children. There aren't many educators around, and we do have to work and take care of the children at the same time, so we end up sending them to schools. And that is a big problem.

K: I know that is a problem. So we are trying to find out how to deal with all these problems, such as whether the school should be residential, yet not be isolated. It is not just that you and I will settle the whole problem in an hour. We cannot. But if you are interested and I am interested, we can together create this thing.

Q: I have found an answer for myself because I believe that I am responsible for my three children. I have taken them every three to four years to a different environment, a different culture, and I have experienced that culture with them. And so I am released. They are transformed. I experience it for myself with them, but I have found I have had to do a lot travelling!

K: Sir, that does not solve it. You are missing the point. Does showing your children different cultures, different societies, different ways of thinking solve the problem?

Q: No, the problem is solved by the experience of seeing and being involved with the situation, then coming back for the inward education. Addressing the question that you asked about the possibility in our life to educate ourselves inwardly and outwardly, the outward I find in the travel, in the cultures, in the different religions or beliefs and ways of living.

K: I understand that, sir.

Q: And then the inward is how we are able to relate between ourselves to it, or for ourselves individually.

K: I understand that, sir, but this is a much wider and deeper problem because we may not be able to travel. We may be living in a village, in a town, confined, and we have not too much money. It is not just a casual problem that one human being has solved, it is a collective problem, it is a problem for each one of us how to deal with this. We say we are responsible for our children, but I question that.

Q: Responsibility is instructing the children and learning ourselves with them.

K: Madam, you say you are responsible. Are you? What does responsibility mean?

Q: You are responsible only when you love, that is the only responsibility.

K: What does the word *responsibility* mean? Please, go slowly into this.

Q: The ability to respond directly to what is happening.

K: That is, adequately. That means that if you do not respond adequately, there is conflict. Responsibility means to respond totally to the problem of the child and the parent. If you feel utterly, totally responsible for the child and therefore love the child, you want to educate him not to be killed or kill, but you don't. Let's not go into all that because it is a tremendous problem.

So our question is: for what reason do you want the child to be educated? Why are you all educated? What for? You have been to schools, colleges, if you are lucky, or university, what for?

Q: To be free of conditioning. (Laughter)

K: You are further conditioned, aren't you? In all the colleges and all the universities and all the schools that exist now you are conditioned. So education must have a different meaning, mustn't it. And that means education implies cultivating the totality of man, the outward, intellectual, emotional, sensitive, and also cultivating a mind that is capable of seeing something real, true. All that is implied. And we are saying that no school, no college or university is doing that. They may do a master's degree in something, but they are not concerned because it would lead to tremendous danger.

Q: Krishnamurti, you spoke of the possibility of educating a man totally. Is it possible in educating man totally externally to automatically learn of everything within, or in learning of everything within, to automatically have a knowledge of everything without?

K: (Laughs) You know this is a battle that has been going on between the commissar and the yogi. (Laughter) The commissar says to pay attention to everything external, arrange everything properly outwardly, control, subjugate it through tyranny; arrange everything first outwardly and then if you have time, think about the inner. And the yogi says not to bother with the outer, but begin with the inner—and he disappears into the woods or joins a community. So this battle has been going on throughout the ages. We are saying it is neither that nor this, it is the totality; it is the whole, do not break up the whole as the outer and the inner.

Q: You are going to build a school and you say that all the universities in the United States don't teach you right, so I am going to teach you right.

K: Oh, no, (Laughs) I don't say that, sir. For the love of Pete, I am not saying that.

Q: What you are saying is that by admitting we do not know something, we can begin to learn about it.

K: Sir, look, to learn about physics, I must go to a scientist who knows about physics. I must go to a man who knows mathematics to learn mathematics. I learn, and that becomes my knowledge. Now please listen to this carefully. Is there *anyone* who can teach you about inner knowledge? Only when there is no authority will you learn about yourself. There must be the authority of knowledge as a scientist. He teaches you what he knows and therefore he becomes the authority. A good doctor tells you what to do if you are unhealthy because he has studied medicine, practised, spent years and years, and he has accumulated knowledge and he becomes the authority. If he is a good doctor, he talks it over with you and he tells you what to do, and you follow it. Now, is there any authority for inward understanding of yourself? If you have an authority for that, then you are merely following the authority, not

understanding yourself. This is simple enough! Therefore
I say, authority has its place as knowledge, but there is no
spiritual authority under any circumstances. The gurus, the
priests, the churches, the temples, the whole thing is based
on authority. And that is one of the factors of degeneration of
the mind. We carry the outward authority about mathematics
to inward authority.

Q: It is important to learn, not how to be free but the importance of it, from someone who is already free.

K: All right, sir, just a minute, go into it. Suppose you are free,
and I want to learn from you that freedom.

Q: No, I cannot give it to you.

K: No, then what will I do?

Q: We can together talk about the importance of it.

K: We are doing it now! (Laughs)

Q: All right. If I am free, then it has meaning to discuss it, but
if I am not free and you are not free then how can both of us
become free together?

K: By both realising that we are not free. (Laughter) Of
course, sir. And in going into it, having a dialogue, discussing
it, observing it in our relationship, in our action, everything,
we find out.

Q: Wouldn't it require an extraordinary energy to maintain
an honest inquiry and not degenerate through the focus of
our conditioning?

K: It does, sir, it does. So how do you get that energy?

Q: By wanting to be free.

K: Do you want to find out how?

Q: Yes, how?

K: The moment you ask how, you want a method and therefore
you are back again into the degenerative process of thinking.

But if there is no *how*, what will you do? This is a central issue, do please pay attention to this a little bit.

Q: We talked about relationship a while back and this has to do with learning. How does one achieve a moving relationship in an educational setting?

K: First of all, sir, let's be clear. There is a method to learn mathematics. If I want to learn mathematics there is a definite method. That is simple enough. Now, can I learn about myself through a method? And who is going to give me the method? The guru, the psychologist, the analyst, the priest? And will following the method help me to understand myself? Or I must look at myself; I must be free to look at myself? That means I must be free of all authority to look at myself. Therefore I must be free of the guru, the priest, the psychologist, everybody, and learn to look at myself. That gives me tremendous energy because I have got rid of all the superficial, unnecessary and destructive barriers.

Q: So you feel that if you really desired that enough you wouldn't have to ask how?

K: Sir, again why haven't you got that? You see if you have that intense desire you will get it. Why haven't you got that? You are going off all the time.

Q: If you want the knowledge of yourself, then you must have some idea that that knowledge of yourself is attainable. Therefore you need an experience of some kind to at least get you in that direction.

K: So you take drugs.

Q: Okay, let's say you take drugs and you get that experience and then you look into yourself somehow.

K: No, sir. Why do you want to take drugs? What is happening in the world? The young people are taking drugs; as the old people are taking alcohol, tobacco, so the young people take to different kinds of drugs because they say they want to have a different kind of experience that will help them to have an experience of reality, uncondition their minds and all the blah that goes with it. Do you know what is implied in the word *experience?*

Q: To go through.

K: The word means to go through, but it means something else too. To experience implies recognition, doesn't it? Do think it over together, sir. I experience something. How do I know what I experience? I can only know it because I recognise it. Recognition implies that I have already had it. Of course. Therefore when I experience through drugs I experience something which I have had, which is my conditioning projected.

Q: What happens when you take a drug and it so disrupts your conditioning, it just disturbs the ego structure so much that you, as you have been, are not anymore, and you can see the world through a different set of eyes?

K: So you take drugs, marijuana or LSD or some other kind, there are so many of them, that it disrupts, breaks down for the time being your ego structure—that's what he is saying— and at that moment you see something totally different. And after a certain period that disappears and so you take to drugs again.

Q: What if you incorporate this experience into your day to day consciousness and no longer need to take the drugs?

K: So, that is, you are incorporating what you have experienced through drugs in your daily life. You are all so childish, sorry!

Q: Sir...

K: Wait, let me finish this, sir. So you incorporate, include something you have experienced which is dead, into your living daily life.

Q: What I mean to say is...

K: Yes, sir, that is simple. I experience through a drug, through mesmerism, through all kinds of ways, something which is free. That experience becomes a memory and I want to live according to that memory, or include that thing in my daily life. A dead thing with a living thing, how can you do it! This is what I have been saying, which is, we are functioning all the time within the field of the known and never free from that. And that is one of the factors of deep degeneracy. Whether you like it or not that's a fact.

Q: Sir, didn't you say once that it took the strength of a genius to overcome circumstances of one's life?

K: I don't know if I said that, but it doesn't matter.

Q: What if older people honoured the question of whether we can educate the total man?

K: I know, sir, that's what I am saying. The gentleman is asking, which we have asked before: how can we educate the totality of man? In schools, in colleges, in universities, in the family, in our relationship intimately, how can this be done? Can we stick to that thing for the time being, please?

Q: I think the point is that one cannot be educated totally as a human being. Perhaps the schools can teach about mathematics or history or something, but that one must learn on one's own self-realisation, I don't think one can be taught that.

Q: As I understood it, first the meeting was to have a dialogue on right education, and then we decided that the way to go into that was to first look at the problem, and then out of that we saw that one of the problems was conditioning of the teacher, the student and the parent. Another problem that seemed to arise in the dialogue was the one of authority of each of those. So that's where we are so far.

K: That's right, sir.

Q: Sir, that brings up a point I would like to discuss: why do we separate our educational environment from the so-called real environment? In other words, why do we have schools which are separate from what is happening in real life?

K: Real life is part of the school, isn't it?

Q: But in most cases it is not, sir. In most cases you go and you hear somebody talk about something and they are not doing it, they are not really involved with it.

K: Of course, sir.

In this dialogue we have talked about authority, unconditioning ourselves and the student, and a relationship not only between the parents and the children but between the educator and the educated. Right, sir? Shall we stick to that for the time being and see what is involved in total education? That is, authority denies freedom, but the authority of a doctor doesn't destroy freedom. And there must be freedom to learn; that is the essence of learning, surely. Freedom. Now, what does that mean? In a school or in a family where we are trying to learn the totality, the cultivation of the whole of human being, what place has freedom and authority? Please listen to this.

Q: So that's one of the problems in a right education to establish the correct...

K: To understand it; for the student as well as the educator to understand what place has authority and what place has freedom. Can the two go together?

Q: That's the question.

K: We are investigating, we are having a dialogue about it. So what does freedom mean? Does it mean every student doing what he likes? Go into, sir. And every student wants that, because he has been conditioned to that: this permissive society, do what you want, individual expression and all that. So he comes with that conditioning and says, 'I am going to do what I want to do. If not, I am going to be violent, vandalize', you know all that follows. So, does freedom mean doing what you want to do? And can you do what you want to do? And what is it you want to do? Express your conditioning freely? (Laughter) Go into it, sir, go into it, play with all this.

Q: Sir, freedom has to exist, and does exist in relationship.

K: Madam, please listen to this first thing. Freedom is absolutely necessary, that is a human demand, historically it is so. And does freedom imply doing what you, as a human being, want to do? That's what you are doing now, isn't it, each one doing what he wants to do.

Q: Is there such a thing as beneficial conditioning?

K: No, all conditioning—you see, conditioning is conditioning, not beneficial. You may call one conditioning beneficial and I might call that evil. So we are talking of conditioning; there is no good, and being better. You know the French phrase, 'the better is the enemy of the good'? Right, let's proceed. Let's see this; please stick to this. Does freedom imply each one doing what he wants to do? Go into it, sir, don't answer me, look at it in yourself. As a human being, does freedom mean doing what you want to do, does freedom mean to choose? And we say freedom implies choice. Right? The capacity to be allowed to choose this, that or the other. Now, choice implies confusion. I don't know therefore I choose; if I am clear there is no choice. Therefore being not clear I choose and therefore deny freedom. Does freedom mean being attached to this, that or the other, which is choice—you understand, sir? I am a Hindu and I become a Catholic because I am free to choose!

Q: But if you are a Hindu and you stay a Hindu then you are conditioned to be one.

K: I don't want to be a Hindu. I am not a Hindu, or a Catholic. But I am just showing to you.

Q: I understand that. What I am saying is that if you were to remain a Hindu then it would be because of your conditioning.

K: Of course.

Q: Just like it would be your conditioning to have the free choice to choose to be a Catholic.

K: I am saying, sir, I am born a Hindu and I am free to choose and therefore I say, 'I won't be a Hindu, I will be a Catholic'. And I think that is the freedom of choice. From one conditioning I go to another conditioning.

Q: Does freedom not involve seeing?

K: We are seeing now, madam, we are making the picture clear. For goodness sake, look at it. So does freedom mean doing what you like, does freedom mean choice, does freedom mean expressing, fulfilling yourself? Doing what you want to do: 'I want to fulfil'. What is the *you* to fulfil? You are the conditioned entity and you want to fulfil according to your conditioning. And that's not fulfilment, you are just repeating the pattern. So does all that mean freedom? Obviously not. Therefore can you as the educator, as a parent, be free of that, not just verbally?

Q: That's the problem.

K: Not a problem. If you see that, sir, you won't be.

Q: I see that for five years sir, I see that point but I can't sustain it.

K: Ah, sir, wait a minute, you can't sustain it. I'll show you, wait, go into it.

Q: Be aware of the fact—that I understand. That I do too. In attention, be aware of the inattention.

K: I'm going to show you something, sir. Once you see this you will understand it quickly. When you see a snake you react instantly. That reaction you don't have to sustain. Whenever you meet a snake you will react always in the same way—why? Because your parents, your society, your books, said that snakes are dangerous. That is your conditioning. That conditioning says the snake is dangerous, and therefore you react. And that conditioning is your sustaining factor. Right? You are following this, sir?

Q: Could you repeat it?

K: Oh, no. I have to repeat it? Sir, you asked a question, how to sustain what you have perceived. You have perceived a snake and you react. That reaction is your conditioning responding. That conditioning is the result of past knowledge, experience; parents have told you that it's a dangerous thing to touch a snake, or your books have told you, so you are conditioned. And that conditioning is the sustaining factor which says to move, run away, leave it alone. Now, is there a sustaining factor when you see all this is not freedom? You understand, sir? No? I see freedom is not choice. Freedom is not to do what I want. Freedom is not fulfilling myself.

Q: Freedom is to observe.

K: Wait. Freedom is not authority. Right? I see that. Not verbally, not intellectually but as truth, because I have an insight. I have an insight into the fact that where there is authority inwardly there is no freedom. I see very clearly the truth that the demand for fulfilment is the fulfilment of my conditioning,

and that's not freedom. Right, sir? I see the truth of it and seeing the truth of it is the sustaining factor. I don't have to have
any other factor. Got it?

Q: Didn't you repeat it just now?

K: Of course, if you are not paying attention, as you didn't just
now, then... I have to repeat it ten times. If you pay attention
you'll see it and it is finished; you don't say, 'Well, I must pay
attention to it again', you see the truth of it. When you see a
bottle marked poison, finished; you see it, you don't take it.

So the total education of man implies, for that education
there must be complete freedom, not the freedom which you
have called freedom. Then can you have that freedom in a
school where the teacher, the educator really has seen the
truth of it and therefore helps the student to see it, in conversation, at table? Every moment he points it out, discusses it.
And therefore out of that freedom there is order. You understand, sir?

Q: We relate about encouraging discoveries.

K: We have done this just now. (Laughs)

Q: What do you mean by total education?

K: I am explaining, sir. Seeing, listening, learning about
mathematics, learning what freedom is. Right, sir? So total
education implies the art of learning, to put everything in its
right place: knowledge in its right place. If I don't know how
to drive a car, I learn. I must know mathematics, it's part of
the structure of life. Mathematics means order. The highest
form of mathematics is the highest order in life, not just learning some trigonometry and all the rest of it. And total education implies the learning about authority. And also learning
if there is something sacred in life, not invented by thought
but really something holy in life. Not the things invented by

priests and the statues and the beliefs, that's nothing sacred, it is the outcome of thought. So all this is the cultivation of the whole of the human being.

Q: Sir, can we remember that this is not dependent upon a specific place?

K: To have a school in this beautiful place is marvellous, I am glad we have got it. We are going to have a school here, we are working for it, we have to have money and all the rest of it. This is a beautiful place, we will do it, but it can be in other places.

Q: By education do you mean right living in and out?

K: Of course, sir.

Q: Sir, I am not sure this is completely relevant but I really hope it is. I heard you once say that freeing the mind is a different action. There are two different actions required, one if you are partially confused and one if you are completely confused. Two different actions.

K: No, sir. No, there is no partial confusion and complete confusion. Either one is confused or not confused, there is no partial confusion.

Q: Where do the parents, Mr Krishnamurti, fit in with what we have talked about?

K: I'll show you. Sir, we want the parent to be part of the school, the parent must be interested in what we are learning, what we are doing, otherwise he is not a responsible parent. It's like sending off a child and getting rid of it. We are saying the parent, the teacher and the student are all concerned with this.

Q: Isn't right or wrong a matter of social conditioning?

K: Of course it is. If you go to India, they think it is very bad to do certain things which you consider quite normal here.

That is their conditioning and this is your conditioning. But the good is not conditioning. What is good is not good here and bad over there; what is good is good everywhere. And that good, which means the goodness, the flowering of that goodness, the beauty of that, is not to be touched by thought. Thought can't produce goodness.

6

CAN WE CREATE AN ATMOSPHERE OF TOTAL NON-ACTION?

Krishnamurti (K): I have been reading something about whales and elephants, especially the whales. They have had complete security and safety. Nothing could attack them, destroy them, and man has come along and he is destroying them. This is just a discussion, I am not laying down anything. If there is complete security, in the deep sense of that word, we can create a mind that is extraordinarily stable. As we are going to start afresh with a totally new school, I feel a sense of great security and vast inward protection is going to give the student an extraordinary capacity. I have been talking about this in India for forty years, but nobody has paid any attention. Can we give that security and have a protective freedom in which the mind can function—not personally, not isolated, selfish and so on—but be a mind that is full, rich and whole? Could we have those two elements: complete security and great protective freedom? We will discuss what those two involve. Then the curriculum, what to teach, how to teach, will all come in relation to those two. You see, then, where you teach matters more than the content of what you are teaching. Where do you teach?

Questioner (Q): How do you mean, where?

K: The place, the ambience, the environment, the atmosphere, the sense of seriousness, holiness. All this matters a great deal more than the subject matter of what you are teaching. Not that the subject matter isn't important; it does matter but it takes second place in relation to the whole thing. Can we have the security, protection and, not in the sense of within four walls or the garden, but the atmosphere?

John Lilly has been experimenting with dolphins and whales. They have enormous brains, and apparently from what the researchers say, they are capable of teaching man something which man does not know. They are highly sensitive and learn very quickly, I think because they are so completely secure. Nothing attacks them. There is no danger to them. The dolphins are not usually aggressive. They are very docile, very affectionate.

Q: Do you think that this atmosphere of security, the feeling of security...

K: Security, protection and an atmosphere in which to learn. If your child was completely secure, had no fear, was protected in the sense of having freedom and yet being watched over, I am sure that would create a different mind altogether.

I don't know if I may be a little bit personal. Forgive me. When they found those two boys [Krishnamurti and his brother Nitya], in about 1909, they saw to it that they were protected, because of instructions from "masters" and so on. You may not believe it, but they believed in it. No crown prince was so protected as those two! Their food, their clothes were watched over. When they travelled in a regular carriage, it was the central carriage with two people on either side. I won't go into it, but I am sure that makes a tremendous difference.

Can we create this atmosphere? Because then the boy or the girl is not afraid; the element of fear doesn't enter, and fear is one of the factors of conditioning. Fear as reward and punishment does not enter into it at all. Because the child is protected there is nothing to frighten him, nothing to punish him, nothing to reward him. Can we produce that? I think that is the first thing we ought to discuss.

How do we set about doing it? If you think this is right, if you think it is rational, sane, not some romantic nonsense, if you see that is the right thing, the true thing, then how do we set about it? That means where you teach matters enormously, the atmosphere, the house, their rooms, the space, everything.

Can we create that? And then from that you establish a relationship with the students which is different. They are not afraid of you, therefore they have confidence, trust, and all the rest follows. They know that you care much more than their parents, because your whole time is devoted to it. If you think this is true, then how do we create this thing? How do you create the sense of stability, security?

Q: Sir, it seems there are several elements involved. One you mentioned is being available to the student all the time.

K: Ah, I am not talking about the student at all. Sorry. I am asking you how you will create the sense of total security so that the moment he steps into that place, he knows, he feels that.

Q: I have been in an environment that gave that feeling, and it might be useful to look at places that have that feeling. Maybe others here have experienced environments like this.

Q: I certainly have, but what would you say brought that about? What was the quality or what was the thing that generated the quality? Can one say at all?

K: Not rules. Yes, how was it brought about?

Q: Well, it should be quiet; that implies soft materials. I think it should be warm, I think there should be good light quality but not too bright.

K: Sir, I have been in places like that. They are good, but they have not got the quality of what should be a real home. I do not see how the students are going to walk in the first day to an empty house that has this feeling; that could happen but it is going to be the people who are populating this building, this school, the parents, the teachers and so on, who will create this atmosphere.

You are there. Perhaps three of you are there. What makes the students feel that they are secure? What is the thing they meet? I am a student. What is the thing I want to feel the moment I enter that door?

Q: Well, he obviously meets the appearance of the place, and sees whether it is quiet, harmonious looking, if it is beautiful, if it is not in any way unpleasant to the child.

K: It would be all right, sir, if there was a marvellous tree in a green field and a few of us met there, with the openness, the beauty of the tree, the sky, the fields. But it is not going to be quite like that. They are going to meet two or ten of you. They are going to meet you in the place you have carefully calculated to produce the effect. But it is *you*. Later on it is the floor, the lights. The first impact is *you*. Now, how will you meet them and make them feel this sense that there is an umbrella?

Q: You wholly attend to them in that moment.

K: That doesn't quite satisfy me; I want to penetrate more deeply into it. What is it you are trying to do with the student? Not what the student is trying to do with you, but what is it you are doing? What is it you are actually doing with that boy or girl? Not only at the moment they enter, but during a whole ten or fifteen year period, what is it you are trying to do? If I were here permanently, I would then work at it; but as I am gone, what is it you are all trying to do?

Q: Isn't it to provide the opportunity for people to become free, for these children to become whole and free, and for us to become whole and free ourselves, become deconditioned?

K: That is just it. That is a later movement. I am questioning the whole thing. What is that child being shaped into? I am using the word *shaped*, not conditioned, not moulded. What is it that is being born in contact with you?

Q: I know one or two people who gave me that feeling when I was young in school, who made me feel that everything was all right just as it was. They were not full of worry. There was nothing I was supposed to do that I didn't know about that I should know about. They weren't in the process of being anything other than what they were.

K: Would you say I was doing nothing? The student enters and I meet him, and I am doing nothing.

Q: It sounds pretty good! I think there has to be a kind of seriousness of ongoing activities.

K: Of course. I am not bothered about that.

Q: You mean, sir, meeting the child, not necessarily as the director or principal or whatever; not necessarily full of questions and things that you want to discuss or bring out, but just meeting the child as she or he is?

K: No, you on your part are doing nothing. Just play around with it a little bit. A flower is in the air. The air is doing nothing to it; it is doing something, but it does not set about doing something.

Q: Wilfully.

K: Wilfully, consciously, unconsciously. Now—I am just investigating, something comes out in talking it over—can I meet the child with complete non-action? Would the child then feel, 'By Jove, here is a man who does not want me to do anything, this way, that way, the other way'?

Q: The child would drop all his defences.

K: Watch it. It is happening. For the first time in the child's life, here is a man who doesn't tell him anything to do and not do. There is danger in that. If you use that as the means of wiping away his troubles, then that is a total barrier; if it is a calculated, controlled, unconsciously desiring to produce a result, then it is gone.

Q: Then there is nothing, because it is doing something.

K: It is a new school. Naturally I feel about this, you see? It is a new school, new ground, a lovely place. Can this be brought about? In doing nothing is the greatest stability. I did nothing to myself; there was no 'I must not be, I must be', or 'This should be'. Nothing! Which does not mean I vegetate, it does not mean I degenerate. The other factor brings degeneration, with all its conflict. Can we do this? Wouldn't the non-action produce a great sense of wholeness? I come into this room, and there you are. You are not blank. You are wide open-eyed. Everything is alive in you. And you do nothing. Wouldn't that produce a relationship with a student who comes from an environment that is always chasing him, threatening him, bullying him? Wouldn't that make the student feel, 'Here I am!

Here is something totally new which I had not expected before, which I never had before'. Therefore his whole activity is different. He doesn't battle you. Is this right?

Q: It sounds right.

Q: Sir, I have seen some students who would take a while to feel these things. They are so dull.

K: Yes, they are dulled, made heavy by drugs, by society. But I am talking for the moment about the teacher who is in the school. Can the woman and the man in the school have this sense of total non-action, which becomes the most positive action? I don't know if you follow this. We can do all this together.

Now, do I understand what non-action means? Does the teacher understand it? The school must be non-active also. The school therefore must have the right proportions.

Q: I don't know if I can do this.

K: No, no. You cannot do anything.

Q: We have to be careful not to form an action about inaction.

K: Yes. We are talking about protection and an action and a stability which is non-active.

I'm sorry to have mentioned those two boys. I must finish that. There were instructions about how to deal with those boys, from on high—if you believe in all that. I am not being cynical or sceptical. [Those around them] believed it; I am not condemning them. They believed it and therefore they said the boys must be protected, they must have the right food, they must have the right clothes, they must see the right people, they must talk correctly. Everything was laid down.

Q: They were what I would call very pushed about.

K: Oh, very pushed about! They were told to read Ruskin, read about Ulysses, see the cathedrals, go to the theatre, meet the

important people. I am not saying we should do that. We cannot do that, but could we create this atmosphere of total non-
action? Therefore the child is completely at home. Wouldn't
you feel at home if there was nobody telling you what to do,
nobody pushing you around, no husband or wife saying do
this, don't do that, nagging, pushing? Wouldn't you? So why
couldn't the students do that, feel at home, which is their
security?

Q: Doesn't that imply having to choose the children with great
care, because a child who is not sensitive would interpret that
as a vacuum into which he will move?

K: Yes. I do not want to go to the child or the parents yet. I am
concerned only about whether we can create that.

I think that if you are non-active you become very sensitive, naturally. And therefore you see the students as they are,
and you see the whole background so you deal non-actively
with them. You see, if you are non-active, then I expose myself;
I don't mind because you are not going to criticise me, you are
not going to threaten me, you are not going to punish me. I
expose myself, and so you see me. And it does create an atmosphere. It does create some potential. But, you see, no school,
no college or university or family provides this; therefore it
is like the wave in the sea. Nothing threatens the student.
Nothing. No punishment. That does something extraordinary. It must. Do you see the truth of this? The truth, not the
verbal reality. If you really see, then it is finished. Then we
can go on and say: how are we non-actively going to teach the
students mathematics, or history or any subject? How would I
non-actively teach you mathematics?

A little boy learns that history is crime, murder, wars, and
about the heroes of those wars. I teach you history to deny

totally all that. That is negation. Non-actively I teach him history so that he sees the truth of what man is in his relationship to society, to property, to power, position, all that—which is history.

Q: It is not from any point of view, but rather taking the whole of man, let's say the culture of man.

K: And the culture of man is this: wars, power, position, chicanery, dishonesty. That is our history. And the heroes of that history are the most dishonourable people. So, in teaching I would bring out the negation of all that. I would say, look at—say Washington. He was the one of the richest men at the end. I would talk about all that non-actively, not trying to convince the student of anything, because I see the whole thing as a reality of thought, which has no... I see it, and therefore I say it is nothing. I can read history and say it is nothing. That is the reality. King Henry VIII existed, but it is nothing.

Q: History as it is taught in schools today is connected to the social system, so you do not learn that Washington was a wealthy man at the end of his tenure. You would learn that he is the father of your country, because history is used to manipulate so that you will come out of school and mesh nicely into the social system.

K: They twist actuality to suit their own national vanity. How would I teach mathematics non-actively?

Q: Well, the root of all mathematics is order.

K: So I would talk about order. Order is non-active, and therefore it is orderly. The higher you go into mathematics, the more orderly the mind must be. I can invent a lot of ways of teaching, can't you?

Q: It seems to me that it must be experienced. A lot of mathematics and science and everything can just be taking place, and the child can be joining in. And then you explain to the child how mathematics and science are used.

K: They learn very quickly. I would also help them to listen non-actively. There is tremendous possibility in this, sir. Begin with listening. To listen properly, the school must begin with quietness. Before I teach mathematics, I would say, 'Sit still, be quiet. Think what you like but be quiet. Sit still, because then only can you listen to what I am going to tell you. But if you come rushing in, pick up a book and I start, you do not listen. Be quiet. If you want to look out of the window, look out. But look. Look and give your attention to what you are looking at'.

Q: You have a whole life there.

K: We will create a school that has never existed before.

Q: The remarkable thing here is that we are doing this with the younger child. After they get to high school age…

K: It is more difficult.

Q: Much more difficult.

K: Now, can you convey this to the teachers? They are important, not the children.

Q: Well, they are the ones who are responsible.

K: They are. Can you convey this to the students? They will eat out of your hand. Absolutely. They will do anything you want. I would. Because you are really caring.

Q: There are some children who never get it.

K: What do you do with those children at your school?

Q: Some we stay with as long as a year and a half, and others we just let go. It is very difficult. It takes a lot of patience.

K: Yes.

Q: Have you learnt now, in the experience you have had at your school, to be able to sense which children will be able to open up to this, or isn't it that predictable?

Q: Well, we have made a lot of misjudgements, but I think we are getting better at it. I don't know if I can describe it.

K: Sir, how do you judge? You have two or three other teachers, half a dozen of you. How do you judge?

Q: Mostly through feelings, but the procedure is to interview the child with the parent. We tell them about the school and show them slides of the school to give them a sense of it. Then we talk to them about themselves, and we come to some sort of consensus based upon our feelings about the child.

K: Now, how do you come to that consensus?

Q: It comes through knowing. Sometimes we are wrong and sometimes we are right.

K: Sir, here we are, several of the teachers. I am the student. Each one of you is going to vote. If three of you disagree and the majority agree, then what do you do?

Q: It never comes out that way, because we keep talking until we all agree, one way or the other.

K: So it must be unanimous?

Q: Yes.

K: Right. Then how do you bring about this unanimity? Through talking?

Q: Talking about our feelings.

K: Talking about the student, and not in front of the student. You say, 'Please go outside and play', and between yourselves how do you do it? Talk about our feelings with regard to the student?

Q: There are two ways we do it. At the beginning of the year we do it that way, and if the child comes in the middle of the year, we have him or her visit for three days.

K: But even then, what is the process of your casting the vote of unanimity or disagreement? How do you produce it? By talking?

Q: Yes, we just say what we think about the child or feel about the child, whether we think the child will fit in or not.

K: Sir, can you find another way? Because in talking about him, when I talk to you, I express my feelings. I may not be honest with myself. Because you are running the show, if I accept your view but inside there is a tension, it will manifest itself later on in my disliking the child. Can this be avoided?

Q: Well, we work pretty hard at it. We haven't totally avoided it, but we work pretty hard on keeping ourselves clear with each other. If we have considerations and reservations about each other we share them.

K: No, I'm attacking it. Sir, there are four of us. The student comes. I know his father, his mother, whether they are a good family, have money or no money. I know him because I have read a report. I have talked to the parents, seen their language, their attitude, the way they sit, the way their house looks, their pettiness, their meanness. I know all that. Can I be free of all the prejudices which I have about that, deliberately put aside my prejudices. We deliberately say, 'I am not going to let my prejudices, my feelings, my respectability, my snobbishness, or egalitarian outlook interfere with this'. I deliberately put away all that, and you do that, and they do that. Then when we are totally unanimous, there is no restriction, there is no secretiveness, there is no suspicion, there is no authority. All that is wiped out. Then we three or we ten look at the child quite differently. It is a total look, not your look and my look.

Q: Yes. It is non-active then.

K: Yes. It is the look of all of us who have no prejudice. Therefore it is non-active and so on, and our judgment will invariably be right. That is real clairvoyance, sir. Then the student shows me everything—if we all agree. If the parent comes in a Cadillac and another drives up on a bicycle, we look without the cycle, without the Cadillac.

(Pause)

Well, sir, where is your curriculum?

Q: I think with understanding this, I have no curriculum to present at all, I have nothing to offer. We want to get the teachers several months ahead so that we can sit down and fundamentally discuss all of these things. We will produce an understanding of the substance of the school. History and mathematics are easier to discuss, but then you get into some of the more difficult ones such as language and art. Not science, but art, subjects that straddle the factual and the non-factual side. You can teach form and order and proportion and symmetry, but how do you teach good taste or how do you convey good taste?

K: I think, sir, good taste you can teach.

Q: You can teach it?

K: Of course. I come into this house and I see immediately there is good taste, because I am sensitive, I want to learn. I'm sorry, I'm not snobbish, but I go into another home and I see there is no taste at all. And I see how a student is dressed, whether it is in good taste. You can teach me—but you can't teach me beauty.

Q: To find an art teacher who has this sense is something rare. They all want to throw pots, paint watercolours. They feel that is art. That all has to do with what they feel is creativity. They want the children to express themselves, you know, to be something.

K: Sir, unless you create a sensitivity, I won't learn anything, even mathematics. And art is much more difficult. Unless I am sensitive to beauty, I just paint, I just copy. When I produce a ceramic, it looks a new kind of shape or a new colour but that is... So how are you going to bring this sensitivity to a child?

Q: Sir, we have done a lot of this, exposing students to museums or where they have an opportunity to participate, taste things. Do they change, do they learn?

K: I am asking a different question: are they sensitive?

Q: You just keep exposing them to a lot of things, then it comes out.

K: Yes. So you are saying, take them to museums, expose them to the best pictures, the best music, best of everything; expose them and that will bring out their sensitivity, or wipe away the crust.

Q: Something like that, only we don't concentrate on museums.

K: No, no, I am taking that as an example.

Q: In my experience, you take them around to a lot of places, and you provide this non-active environment and this kind of support, without making judgments, and then this curiosity begins to come back.

K: How will you bring this about? If I do not have it, you can take me to all the museums in the world and I will be damned silly at the end of it. How will you bring about this sensitivity in me when you see the importance, the necessity of being sensitive, not only to pictures; to everything?

Q: By living it.

K: No, wait, just a minute. I come in as a student. I do not know what you are talking about when you say *sensitivity*. I am sensitive when I put a pin in myself, or see a new car, but I am not sensitive to all the glory around me, or the hideousness, whatever it is. How will you awaken this?

Q: By continuously communicating to them my own sensitivity.

K: How?

Q: By pointing it out: 'Oh, look at that bird, look at that ani-mal, look at that, feel the sunshine'.

K: Sorry, forgive me. I listened the other night to Kenneth Clark saying a certain picture is the most marvellous thing you have ever seen. He was doing propaganda for that pic-ture. And I said, 'To hell with this man, I can look at the picture!'

Q: He was giving you a critic's point of view and all the knowl-edge that goes with it. Why isn't that relevant? Isn't that interesting?

K: Because he is not totally sensitive; he is sensitive in one direction.

Q: Well, who is totally sensitive?

K: Ah, I am concerned with the total sensitivity. I am con-cerned with sensitivity to the whales, to the birds, to the poor people. I am sensitive all round. That is what I want, not just a lop-sided sensitivity. I am asking how you will bring enormous sensitivity, with the depth of that word. How would you do this? It is one of your problems.

Q: If you say, 'Oh, see the hawk', or something, is that…

K: No, you call me when I am doing something and say, 'Come and look at that hawk'. I rush and look at that hawk, but that is a different thing. I wonder if by talking, by example, you can bring this sensitivity. I have talked a great deal in these schools. I have said, 'When you are walking don't pick up the branch and strip the leaves off it, don't pull it all out and leave the empty stem'. Several times I said not to do it. Nothing en-ters. So, what will you do? No example. Just see this as an ex-ploratory business, not agreeing or disagreeing—no example, no talking, because if you talk then you are creating a feel-ing that you are sensitive and the student is not, that he must somehow come up to your level. How will you do this? I want to find out. May I go into it?

I would go into the question of attention, what it means to attend—forget sensitivity—what it means to look, what it means to hear. Then you will have it. If you are teaching me something, I do not want to be taught; then our relationship is different—example, talking—then we are at a different level. But if you go into the question of attention, then you and I are both trying to find out. When Maria [Mary Zimbalist] calls me, 'Look at that hawk', I really want to see, because to me attention is something I talk a great deal about. To me, that is the clue to non-action or whatever it is.

So when the students come into the class, I'd say, 'Sit quietly', and I'd say, 'If you do not want to sit quietly, look out of the window, but *look*, give your attention to that. Don't say, "Oh, I mustn't look, I must study". If you want to talk to the boy next to you, talk'. I am not going to prevent you from talking.

Q: Sir, you used to say these things year after year at Rishi Valley School, and inevitably after a talk students would go off to classes and would ask questions and so on. They would say, 'Krishnaji says this and says that', and then we would have a staff tea and these things would come up again. But the question of attention or listening was not pursued further with the teachers, whose responsibility it was.

K: No, of course not. They were not interested.

Q: Well, unless they explore this for themselves, to hear what you say on these subjects will not mean anything.

K: So, sir, how do we put the house together? Because on Friday we are going to meet the architects. Bearing all this in mind—non-action in teaching mathematics, history, art, the whole curriculum—what kind of room, place, house, roof, wall, will give the feeling of all that? The architects here are American; if we were in Europe they would be European, but you do not want a European, American or a Japanese school, you want one where all these things are involved: good taste, good depth, curtains that are very good, bricks that have life in them.

Q: I would refer back to the time when we met the students who want to come into the school, and we all dropped our prejudices and our good taste and everything else, and then we came sort of clearly to something.

K: I understand, sir, but we have both to face the arguments the day after tomorrow, and the Foundation has told the architects to go ahead, build, produce. We will get the money and the design, so we must...

Q: There must be a series of meetings, there must be a kind of language that we are working from that includes the architecture. We must school ourselves, and start talking through these things and then recording them so that they can be transmitted to the architect.

K: They will be here the day after tomorrow. We will talk to them, tell them what we want, we will go into all this. I would like to be there because I feel it is something new, and I want— not '*I* want'—to help them to create the right place. If we had not been there, they would have put the road right round and the buildings would have been in that meadow. How do we do this, sir? I feel—not '*I* feel'—every brick matters; I feel that way about the beams, the handles, the hinges.

Q: Well, that is called supervision; it means being there.

Q: It means also planning it all, going into, being aware of every detail about the place, the concept all the way down the line.

K: So, are we saying amongst ourselves that we will talk to them and tell them everything that we feel, as much as we can? And then we say, 'From what we want, what we feel, go ahead, show us all of it, draw something'.

Q: Krishnaji, if I may interrupt. What we asked them to do, because you are leaving Sunday, was to very informally, loosely, give us the direction of their own thinking, and to propose what they have thought. And then we will react and they will see what everybody says. This is the first time all this has been discussed.

K: I know, but what I want to get at is that when we are gone somebody here has to watch what they propose step by step, and be constantly in communication with us about the building.

7

WE MUST BRING ABOUT A PSYCHOLOGICAL CHANGE IN OURSELVES

Krishnamurti (K): I think it might be worthwhile if we can start as though we are starting from now, a clean slate.

The principal of Rishi Valley school in India was at Brockwood for three weeks and we spent every morning discussing what the school in Rishi Valley should be. If I go over it with you, it might be worthwhile. We said that from the age of 4 or 5, up to 12, the chief concern should be psychological change in the student, to uncondition him, his behaviour, his way of speaking, his outlook. Not only psychological change, but also reading and writing and all that. So from the age of 5 to 12 we would have students or children who are not being conditioned in a new way, but the chief concern of the teachers would be to see that psychologically, inwardly, they are totally different from their environment, from other children, society, so that when they grow up, after 12, they still retain that quality. After the age of 12 to 18, some of them may go to university, others may not. We left it at that for the time being.

Here we are concerned with students or children from 5 to 12. Please, we will discuss this; I am not laying down any law; I am no authority. I abominate authority, so I would like to add here that there should not be a division between the trustees and the teachers. After all, they are concerned with the school with us. The trustees are responsible to the government, if I may point out, and to me. They are concerned with the school. They are concerned with what the Centre should be, which we will discuss later on. The trustees are concerned with the whole thing. It is not you and we. If there has been any division, it was a misunderstanding and that misunderstanding should be wiped out. We are all together in this, in the same boat, and we are concerned with how to bring about a psychological change in the 5 to 12 year olds.

I think that for administrative purposes there must be a head as there is at Brockwood. But if you are the head you are not somebody apart, dominating us. We are together creating the school, and therefore together we as the teachers are responsible to the Foundation and the Foundation is responsible for us. There is no division.

Questioner (Q): I think that is clear. If anybody does have a question, I think now is the time to raise it because there have been misunderstandings.

K: Please ask, and we will go step by step with it. Once the trustees and we all agree, the confidence is there, confidence from the trustees in you if you are all working together. But we have to show that we are capable and that they are welcome to help us. Wherever I have been, there has been a battle. There are trustees of the Foundation in India, and trustees in England, and people say they are separate, but I have fought it. So there is no division between the trustees and the teachers.

We are together in the same boat. The trustees have a certain function, to see to publishing books and arranging talks; and the teachers have their own responsibility; but we are all working together and not separately. Please, let's make this quite clear so that there is no misunderstanding between the trustees and the group who are going to take charge of the school. We are together.

Q: May I make a plea about this, because I have seen it in the other Foundations? That is, if there is something that seems like a misunderstanding or a disagreement, it should immediately be brought up. You go to the person or the people and say, 'Am I right in thinking that you think this?' Undo it right away, because often if, for reasons of tact or letting something go by, there is a tiny misunderstanding and it is left there like a pebble in your shoe, from that grows further misunderstandings. It is so easy to just do the human thing and say, 'Look, am I wrong or right about this?' We can do this, because we are a group, among ourselves.

K: Quite right.

Q: It is terribly important that we speak normally like friends so that there won't ever be misunderstandings. Do not assume that somebody thinks this about that but find out right away.

K: Yes. So now let's start.

Do you think it is possible from the age of 5 to 12 to educate children not only academically but much more, laying emphasis on the psychological movement and change in that movement? I think that is very important not only in the present situation in America but it is a real problem of human beings.

Q: Is there something arbitrary about the age of 12? Is it going to be different after age 12?

K: No, put it any age you like. When discussing with the head of the Rishi Valley school, we said from 5 to 12. If you say that is not suitable here, that it will be 5 to 10, or whatever, we will agree.

Q: Is it not the case that in any educational forum, whether it is with age 5 or 12 or 18, the same effort is being made?

K: Yes, that's right.

Q: I think we are talking about up to junior high school here.

K: This is something which has never been tried. No school has done it, either in India or in Europe or here. This is the first time we are trying to be concerned primarily with the psychological change of a human being. Add academic things during or after, but our primary emphasis is on that.

Q: Is the question whether all of us have sufficient drive?

K: That is one question: sufficient energy, sufficient capacity; and are you really interested in changing the human mind? Not only the students but ourselves in relation to the student? Not that we must change first and then teach the children, but together we are changing each other.

Q: Sir, I think we need more people. We need more trained teachers, we need people to...

K: If you need them, how are you going to get them? To what extent will they go with you? Will they go with you entirely?

Q: Well, we have people who are in the wings waiting.

K: But are they involved with other things?

Q: One would have to clear that up first.

K: You see, sir, I don't know if you know enough about all these things. People join various groups and then add this as another feather. It doesn't work that way. They go to get sensitivity training or learn Transcendental Meditation or how to awaken kundalini. I have been through this from childhood, and it is so utterly empty from my point of view: Transcendental Meditation, sensitivity training, going off to Zen Buddhism and trying to meditate. So there are many people who are involved in many of these things and they want to add this too. Therefore they say they are delighted to come here and help, but they keep an eye elsewhere. So we have said at Brockwood, 'Please, we don't want you if you come here to go off for the weekend to meditate with the Transcendental Meditation people'. We have gone into it and said that Transcendental Meditation is sheer nonsense. I explained how it arose in India and so on. So, if people say they like that, we say, 'Perfectly right; go, but to mix it with this doesn't work'.

So do you have the capacity, energy, drive to create such a school? We will invite others. They might come and help; they will join, but we must be a nucleus of people. This is the thing that matters.

Q: How can we know in advance whether we have sufficient drive?

K: Ah, no; but you know the feeling of it, the inward demand for such a thing and the intensity of such a demand.

Q: That comes and goes.

K: Ah, no. It will not come and go if it... Sir, I have to earn money, work for money, but if I say this is the thing which I feel is right, is correct, is true... Because human beings in the world are degenerating; Americans are becoming vulgar. And this should be an oasis. An oasis is a place where there is fresh water in the middle of a desert. That fresh water is kept, not by you and me, but by the spring, which is there. If we say this is the thing that is absolutely necessary, that this should be the primary thing for children in their life in relationship with a teacher, before reading or writing, if you feel that, if we all feel that, then we will have capacity. Because, after all, capacity comes by application. And you can apply when you say, 'This is important. I must do this'.

Q: I want to make one thing clear. We are talking about finding more people to be a part of this new place.

K: Absolutely.

Q: All right. We are talking about teachers, people with practical skills, people who can work with the children on a daily basis, being responsible for them day to day.

K: Teaching them not only to read and write, but psychologically.

Q: Yes, psychologically, academically, socially, all of those things, as you are doing. We are also talking about other people who are not teaching but who are working with the school.

K: In what way?

Q: Well, that is what I want to be clear about.

K: I want to know. Are they interfering or imposing or saying, 'No, sorry, what is important is not psychological change but something else'? Do they want to help the school, but say that we are laying too much emphasis on one thing? Do they come and discuss with you, and because of their capacity and their name and so on, you feel that they know so much more than you do, so you had better kowtow to them? It all depends what they mean by *help*.

Q: Yes, and it depends in what spirit they are part of the school.

K: That is what I am suggesting.

Q: But, sir, I feel that we have in the last six months discovered that we have to have more people on the school side of it.

K: What do you mean by the school side of it?

Q: Well, what I am suggesting is that perhaps we could have a larger, more professional group of people concerned with education.

K: Just go easy on that. I am going to tell you something. Say you, the school directors, and two trustees from the Foundation are going to choose the teachers, the students, the new people who will come and help you. Together you are going to choose. On what basis are you going to choose, select or whatever word you like to use? On his capacity to help us? And what does that word *help* mean? You know how a lot of mischief arises if we are not clear.

Trustee [To a director]: Do you feel that you need a more professional, more qualified advisor to consult with for running the school?

Director: I feel it would be useful to have a bigger group of people who would act as consultants because we are talking about something here that is not like a typical school. We are talking about something that is very complex, to deal with the psychological not just the academic, and I think it would be good to have some sensitive child psychologist or to have someone who had a feeling for this and who could offer insights into things which I am not trained for.

K: You mean a psychologist?

Q: Someone who has gone into these things; not to dominate the group with all of the theory and so on.

K: Find him, if you can find him; and if he's interested in what we are doing, if he says, 'This is right, this is true'; not because he likes you and you like him and all that bilge; if it is the right thing to do, correct thing to do, then of course you will have him. But are there such people?

Q: I just want to know if we are open to this kind of thing.

K: Yes, but first let's be clear that this nucleus of people living at Ojai is primarily interested in a school that is trying to transform the character, the psychology of the student. If that is deeply understood, you can invite anybody. But if they want students to become Zen Buddhists or practise Transcendental Meditation or this or that, I say that is absurd, because we are trying to start something totally new. You might not find such people, but if you find such people, thank God, bring them in.

Q: This does not mean that we are abdicating any responsibility for the children and for the running of the school; it is just something more solid.

K: But there must be a nucleus of people who are here, who are working for this.

Q: I would like to talk about finding teachers.

K: Wait, we will get them, sir, but are you prepared to meet the psychological problem? You have three, five, ten, fifteen students. All right. Are you prepared, do you know, are you aware of how to transform them, how to change their mental structure which is conditioned, which is American? I should think, sir, apart from the number of students, apart from space, we could discuss and see how to meet the problem of change in the student. If that is more or less clear, then we can get other teachers, find space. That will all become a secondary issue. Because this has never been tried. At least I am not aware that any school is concerned with this.

Q: Have your schools in Brockwood and in India not tried this?

K: No. Brockwood started in the first year with giving students freedom to do what they want, because that was the kind of students we had.

Q: It was an older group.

Q: But the intention of the school was to bring about psychological change.

K: Oh, absolutely.

Q: Right. So this has been tried but it hasn't...

K: Ah, no, it has been tried in our schools, but nowhere else. Here we are starting something totally new. Are you prepared for this? Prepared in the sense, do you have the capacity to do what is involved in it, to see what we mean by change, and whether it is possible to change? Can you talk to the students with politeness, consideration, generosity? First, all that. Can you do this? Can we together talk about it, investigate how far we can do it, and how to do it?

Q: Of course we can do that.

K: Let's do that, then. Let's be clear. The trustees of the Foundation and you are one. I want this rubbed in. Sorry! (Laughs) There should not be distrust between you and them. There is no *you* and *them*, you are one. I am saying the Foundation exists to help the school, to see that the school is maintained. In England, the Foundation is helping Brockwood financially. If there is any misunderstanding between the Foundation and Brockwood, they settle it immediately. I want it perfectly clear that there should be no conflict between us, that we will not talk against you behind your back. If we have something to say, we will come and tell you. And if you have something, come and tell us. No backbiting, gossip and all the horror that goes on in institutions.

That is clear. Then the school primarily—not *primarily*; the *only* thing is to change the mentality, the psyche of the student. If we agree that is the essential thing in education, then we will see, now, how to bring this about. Let's discuss it a little bit.

The children come to you very conditioned already, whether they are 5 or 12 or 18. They are rude, especially in

America; they have tremendous energy, do not know what to do; they want to imitate the older people. All that goes on. Now, how would I, as a teacher here, deal with the problem to change their mind, their psyche? How shall I do it? How will you propose to do it?

Q: Is it not first that we must see with clarity what is the nature of their mind?

K: Oh, that is fairly simple, sir, it doesn't take years or a week. You can spot it immediately. I noticed when you were introducing Mrs Zimbalist to one of them, he said, 'Hi', and sat there—in front of an older lady, it is a discourtesy. And you see that. So how will you deal with that boy and say, 'Look, be polite, which means show consideration. If you have no consideration in your heart, you cannot be polite'. How will you help this boy to have this enormous consideration for another, where in America everybody is out for himself? Like the rest of the world, because the rest of the world is copying America, sorry to say. So how will you help that boy to have real consideration for another? That is part of the psychological change. How will you help him? What will you do?

Q: Communicate.

K: Ah, yes, how do you communicate? Come on, sir, we are discussing it. He is against you; he says, 'Why the hell should I get up when I'm introduced?' He is copying the rest. He is already conditioned. He comes here heavily conditioned, and one of the symptoms of that conditioning is discourtesy, lack of consideration. How will you help that boy to have consideration? Follow it, sir, it is very difficult: if you set an example then he is imitating you, either because he is playing up to you or he thinks, 'Marvellous, I'm going to imitate him'. So out of fear, out of affection, out of desire to please you, he imitates you. But that is not consideration.

Q: No.

K: So how will you do it? Go on, sir, tell me. I am one of your students.

Q: I don't know. They resist and that prevents them from going along.

K: Yes. How will you remove the resistance?

Q: You have to deal with it over and over.

K: Then it becomes another habit.

Q: Yes. Sure. And they feel brow-beaten.

Q: Sir, don't you first have to develop some kind of a relationship with them so that they trust you?

K: Now wait, look, that means what? Time. Right? You have them for three weeks, a month or whatever it is, and during that time they are getting strengthened in their conditioning. When you allow time, the older factors become intensified, because they are free here. So what will you do? Let's find out. You can't punish them, give them marks for good conduct (Laughs). You can't say, 'Well, follow me', because here there is no authority. What will you do with that child? Say, 'Please, have the beauty of consideration in you'?

Q: Sir, they don't know what you're talking about when you are using those words.

K: I am talking to myself so that I see they must have it. Of course they are not going to listen to me. I cannot communicate to a dead resistance; they will call me square or this or that, and there it is. So I must be clear in myself how to talk to them so that they feel this, demand it. And there must be a way. Mustn't there be?

Q: I don't know.

K: Ah! Let's find out. Find out. It is a problem, a challenge to you. You say, 'I cannot allow them to imitate me, I cannot exercise authority, I cannot punish or reward them, so what am I to do to awaken in them the utter importance of consideration?' I am only taking that as a symptom of a very profound disease. Now here you are. How are you going to awaken this necessity in that boy? It is left to you; what will you do? You must find an answer. You cannot say, 'Well, I will wait, I will study him'.

Q: Does it make any sense to ask how to find the answer?

K: No. Sir, let me put the question differently. Do you feel—I am not being personal; forgive me if it sounds personal, it is not—do you feel the importance of consideration? Not cultured consideration but the spontaneous feeling that the other person is important too?

Q: Sometimes.

K: Ah, that is not good enough (Laughs). That boy I noticed, he got up. First he had sat down and said, 'Hi', and then presently he felt awkward and got up. So how will you, a teacher concerned with correct behaviour, which means having tremendous feeling for another, how will you do this, if you do not have it? And how will you help the child to have it? If you have it sometimes, he will have it sometimes. So do you feel the importance of this, that one of the factors of human behaviour is consideration, not occasionally but as a flower has a scent? If I do not have it and the student does not have it, how are we going to help each other to have this feeling?

Q: He has to help me also have it?

K: He is my student. I do not have this feeling of it and he does not have it, but together we are going to find out how to get it.

Q: He doesn't want to.

K: Ah! I know, poor chap, he does not, but together we are going to do it because he is your responsibility. Together we are going to have this flower. Now, how shall I do it? It is important for him to have it and it is important for me to have it. How are we together going to have this feeling, because he is my responsibility? What shall I do?

I know what I would do. Think it out, sir. Be open to find out. This is very important to me, because I see the immense dignity of it, the beauty of it; though I don't have it, I feel it is really, profoundly important. Then I have it. You follow, sir? I wonder if you do. If I feel it is profoundly important, it is there. Then—I won't even mention consideration for others—I will say to that boy, 'Forget everything. Sit down'. I would talk to him, not about consideration but about his family, what he thinks, why he thinks. I would go into his mind. Because I feel responsible for that boy, or girl. So I would drill into him. I would let him talk about himself. Then, in talking about himself, he will show that he will trust you. You have opened a door to him, you are a friend. Then you can begin to penetrate.

Q: Sir, doesn't this take time?

K: Ah, don't talk about time. It may take a minute or it may take a day. The moment you introduce time, you are already saying, 'Well, I will get it tomorrow'. I am not interested in time. I see the utter importance of being tremendously considerate, and time is not there.

It is the same with violence. At present, modern civilization is tremendously violent, and those children are violent. So I want to change that; violence must be wiped out of their blood because violence and affection cannot exist together, so I am going to find out how to get totally free of violence.

I do not think you feel the importance of it strongly enough. Sorry. You say, 'I need time. I am not changed and you are not changed'. If you do not feel the importance of being without violence, why don't you? What is wrong with you? Not with *you*, but what is wrong? Why don't we feel revulsion against violence? Not as a reaction; it is something terrible for human beings to have this violence. Why don't we feel it? What is wrong with us? And if *we* don't feel the importance, how do you expect that poor student to?

So it is not a question of time, it is a question of perception, seeing that it is true. I mean, if I am greedy, seeing that; not all the million explanations why I am greedy. I am greedy. If I see the fact, it is finished. In the same way, if I see the absolute beauty and the necessity and the dignity of consideration—really see it as I see a chair—then time does not exist. I will show the boy that, I will talk to him; I will change him; I will spend days at it—not days; but I will spend my energy on that. You see, our tradition says, 'Take time, old boy'. That is our tradition, and I am not a traditionalist. Sorry. It is one of our conditionings to accept a tradition of violence.

So can we and the others who will come to help us do this? The moment you have something real, burning, others will come. You must have the nectar, then the bees will come. If you do not have it, they won't come; you can whistle in the dark. So can we say, 'Look, it is tremendously important for the psychological change of the students that they should have no violence, no word of violence'? If you have it you will see that in no time they will have it.

So can we start with those three children? A school with three children! (Laughs) I love that. Can you start with those three children, bearing in mind that though reading and writing is important, what is far more important is the psychological change? Can we from today be concerned with that and see? Does it interest you, or do you think it is important, that they should change? Not superficially, not having new gadgets and new fashions, but that deeply their minds change. Are you interested in that?

Q: Of course, sir.

K: Now, if you are interested in it, what will you do? How will you approach it? You have three children under your care, who are your responsibility. If you say that is more important than anything else, how will you set about it? This is much more difficult than teaching mathematics, much more difficult than helping them learn to cook. This requires an extraordinary sense of perception, in the sense seeing what the world is, seeing one's relationship to the world, oneself which is the product of the world, as the children are the product of the world, are part of the world. So the child is like me. The child is the product of the world as I am the product of the world, so there is no difference between him and me, profoundly. I am older, taller and all the rest of the nonsense, but profoundly the same movement is at work. Now, can I stop that movement? I don't know what it means to stop it. I don't know what it means to end it. I do not know. And the child does not know. But the child and I are essentially the same: we are the product of this rotten civilization. I see the importance of something. Now, can I communicate this feeling to the child?

Q: Sir, I think for an older child this makes some sense, but for the younger child I don't think they have the capacity to even connect with this.

K: No, I wouldn't even talk about it to the child. They wouldn't even know what you are talking about.

Q: But they can talk about themselves to you.

K: No, I am working at something else. You are missing it. I can talk to those children about consideration until I am blue in the face. They would not even know what that word meant. But I am not talking to those children. They are my responsibility. They are like me. I am not dividing the student and me; we are both the same. What shall I do? It is my responsibility. What shall I do to bring a change? You see, you have not applied your mind to it. That is what I'm pushing against.

Q: One has applied one's mind to this question.

K: Then what? If you have applied, you must have an answer. Sorry, I'm not personally questioning you. If you have applied, it must have shown something. Ah, no, don't say, 'I don't know'. As with anything else, if you apply your mind, you must have an answer. We do not ask the question and find the answer and then apply it. Sorry, I shouldn't be talking all the time.

Q: Sir, isn't this precisely the unique thing about what you generally talk about, such as the stopping of the movement of the "me", that many of us, everyone in this room and thousands of others, have applied their minds at length to that question and have not found an answer?

K: No, because, sir, I think it is that we are not serious enough to ask it. Look, I want to find out the meaning of Ojai. Not the valley; I am talking of the trustees, the school, the whole thing; what is it for? I have found the answer. It will take time to discuss it with all of you, but I have pushed it. My way of pushing is to put the question. I have put it, not because somebody says this, that and the other; I want to find out. I want to find out so I put the question and leave everything else aside. You are telling me what Ojai, the school, ten different things, mean. I listen to you, but the question is so important it keeps the periphery open. I wonder if I am making it clear.

Q: Not that last part about the periphery.

K: The central question is far more important than your answers, but you are not putting the central question.

Q: Which is?

K: Which is: what does Ojai mean? So I am asking you what the school is for. Because I have a couple of children and I need to educate them, therefore, I want a school. But what is the school for? There are a million schools in America.

Q: We know that, don't we? That is what we have been discussing.

K: But do you know it? Or have you been told? Have you said, 'My God, this is the only thing to do'? Do you see the difference? If I had a son, I would be tortured sending him to these rotten schools to turn out like the rest of the million Americans—or Europeans or Indians. So I say now, what shall I do with my son? It would be a tremendous responsibility. I would find an answer. So, if all of us say, 'Look, this is important; we exist as a school, not only as a school but personally and collectively, to see that we are psychologically changed, both in the school and out of it', then you will see what takes place—if that is really, profoundly important.

If you feel that, then you and I can discuss what to do, how to approach the child, who is me. I am not going to study his character; he is conditioned because he is just like me. I have to find an answer for this. So my first question is: are the whole group of us here, trustees and teachers, the lot of us together who are in the same boat, really interested? Not just interested, is it an urgent demand, a challenge, to say that we must bring about a psychological change not only in the students but in ourselves, and therefore in the school, together? I assure you we would create a marvellous school. People will come then. Now, what have you to give? This is something new; they will come if you have something.

8

THE ART OF LISTENING MAY BE THE WHOLE MIRACLE OF EDUCATION

Krishnamurti (K): If we may, I would like to have a dialogue about what correct education is; whether it is possible to cultivate the intellect, the capacity of perception—which is not the intellect; and about what the place of thought is; and whether human minds can ever be unconditioned.

Unfortunately or fortunately, one has been connected with a lot of schools, and apparently it is one of the most difficult things to uncondition the human mind, which has been trained, educated, evolved through punishment and reward. Now we have started a school on a very small scale at Ojai and we are asking if it is at all possible to educate children from age 5 to 12. We will be concerned chiefly with psychological change, which means unconditioning the mind, and finding out, if that is what true education means, how we are to set about it. I would like to have a discussion on that.

Is it possible living in a world that is degenerating, where people are really not concerned with other human beings, to bring this change in the student, not as an idea or as an ideal but actually? Does that mean that the educator must be unconditioned or that the educator unconditions himself and the student as an inner relationship with each other? And is that possible while you are also giving the student an academic background? Can we consider this afternoon how to bring this about? Not through a method; a method implies obviously a conditioning, a system; a sense of conformity to a pattern. So how is this to be done?

Does it depend on the environment? Does it depend on the parents? Does it depend on the quality of the students you have? And does it depend on the educator, feeling the responsibility of this and therefore creating an atmosphere? We tried this in India some time ago, talking to the parents and to the students. It became quite impossible because of the whole economic, social background there. Because of overpopulation they are only concerned with having a good position, getting married, having a house, children, and not getting involved in anything but that. At Brockwood Park in England, we are trying a different kind of education, as we are trying to do here. There they are older students and they come heavily conditioned. If they are American, they have the American background. Many come from Europe or South America, each one with a conclusion, with a moral, with an idea that freedom is to do what you like and non-acceptance of authority—which is excellent in one way but destructive if you do not understand the full meaning of authority.

So we have a tremendous problem if we really want to go into the question of what real education is apart from the technological, academic side of it. We must ask if real education is possible for a human being, conditioned through centuries, with his whole brain structured for survival at any cost, wanting freedom to do what he likes through individual self-centred activity. All that is what we meet. Here we are trying to start a school where the child, the student comes already conditioned. How do we meet that student and convey to him, verbally and nonverbally, our intention? Mustn't we be very clear about what right education is? And because we are clear, though we may not be unconditioned, in relationship with the student can both the educator and the educated be unconditioned? How do we set about this?

First, one has to understand what security is; because most people want security both inwardly and outwardly. If the student does not feel secure in his relationship with the educator, then the problem of conformity, imitation, authority creeps in. So should we consider first what it means to be secure? What does it mean to have total security? Because that is what the students want. They do not get at home; they do not get in relationship with other students. So can we give them complete security, which means they have complete trust? Not, 'I know better than you, therefore trust me', or 'I look after you, protect you, therefore trust me', but give them the feeling that they can rely on you, the feeling that, in their relationship with you, they feel so secure that they are free. Not to do what they like, but the feeling of that very security gives a sense of élan, a sense of freedom, a sense that here are people who are really caring. I think that is one of the major things we should consider. Sorry, I am talking. This is a dialogue.

Questioner (Q): The insecurity breeds conditioning? Is that what you are implying?

K: No. No, we must be careful in usage of the words *secure* and *insecure*. Before we go into the problem of what conditions the mind, we should examine, I think, the meaning of the words *secure, safe.* You must have noticed that children need security; you are educators. And that security takes the form of protection, which any intelligent child would reject. If he has any stuffing in him, he would say, 'For God's sake...' But he must have protection.

Q: Is the security you are talking about the same as love?

K: Not quite. We will go into it presently. Sir, one's brain cannot function efficiently if it does not feel safe, secure. It finds security in some neurotic beliefs; all beliefs are neurotic. So the brain finds security in illusion, in nationality, in "God", in 'I am a Catholic', 'I am a Hindu', I am this or I am that; which are all illusions. The brain demands, insists on having security, and therefore it chooses a particular illusion and lives with that, feeling safe. It may be the family, it may be a position, and so on. The brain has cultivated itself in this area of illusion. All right? Would you accept such a thing? Not *accept*; would you see the truth of it? A Catholic finds tremendous safety, certainty, security in dogma, in Christ, and so on; not only physical security, but intellectual security and economic security. In Italy I must be a Catholic because it pays me; I get a job, and so on.

So can we, as educators, give non-illusory security? What does the word mean? You see, if a child is insecure in the family, if the mother or father leave him, or send him to a boarding school, or are occupied with their own beastly problems, that child is uncertain in his relationship with his parents, as in a broken marriage and so on. That insecurity creates all kinds of fantasies, all kinds of neurotic activity. It has been shown. I think we can accept that as a fact. And the brain must have complete security; only then can it function. So, can we supply this, or help him to have this security, which is not attached to any belief such as, 'I am an American', 'I am English', 'I am a Catholic', 'I am a Communist'? Those are all illusions, non-realities.

Q: Sir, did you say that security is non-attachment to belief?

K: Ah, that us only part of it. Sir, what does security mean to you?

Q: No fear.

K: Yes, but let's proceed; no fear, and no...?

Q: Dependence.

K: Again, what do you mean by dependence? On what do I depend, and why do I depend? Why does one? Why does the child depend? He must depend, but that dependence gradually becomes attachment, with the fear of being alone. I am attached to you and I cling to you because I am basically afraid of being lonely, alone, separate.

Q: Krishnaji, in a young child isn't that dependence healthy in that the child *is* dependent? He doesn't differentiate between neurotic dependency and...

K: That is what I am saying. Can we give him security, and not attachment, not belief, in example, all that? I wonder if I am conveying something to you.

Q: Well, in the young child a lot of the dependency, security is purely physical, just feeling absolutely at home.

K: No, it is physical which gradually becomes psychological.

Q: Later?

K: I am not sure. Don't say later; they are interrelated.

Q: It develops at the same time?

K: At the same time. Look at it, you will see it: 'It's my toy', 'my mother'. You know all this. So they are interrelated. I do not think they can be separated as outside and inside. They both are operating. Tell me, sirs, what is security to you?

Q: Is it a sense of self-worth?

K: Self-worth? That means having confidence in oneself? Would that give you security?

Q: Certainly it seems to.

K: Isn't that separative and divisive, and therefore has a sense of conflict?

Q: It would give you the energy to pursue something.

K: I have confidence in myself that I can write a book, or make money, paint, or whatever one does? Why should one have confidence?

Q: In order to purse an idea. If you did not believe in it or think it worthwhile, you might not have the energy to continue.

K: Isn't it a dangerous thing, to have confidence in oneself?

Q: In the extreme, yes, I think it would be very bad, but somewhere along the line it goes into the mix.

K: Doesn't that cultivate self-centeredness? Is there security in my self-confidence?

Q: Sir, in the young child everything is centred on the child. The whole world revolves around the child; the "I", the "me".

K: That is what I am saying, sir. Does security lie in the "me"?

Q: I think in a young child, it does.

K: Therefore you are emphasizing self-centred, selfish activity, which is what the world is doing.

Q: But it is normal in a young child, isn't it?

K: It is normal, we admit that. We are trying now to find out how to break down that structure.

Q: But if it is in some way healthy for the young child, because he is so small and he only perceives himself as the centre of his world, is it a good idea at that age to try to break that down?

K: No, I agree. Wait a minute, we are discussing all this theoretically. You have a son and the self is beginning to grow, becomes very important, and you tell him to have confidence in himself, to have confidence that he can do this or that, that he can become the President of United States. God forbid. So are you unconditioning the mind, or encouraging a deepening of that conditioning?

Q: Perhaps we should define it.

K: Sir, if I am a painter, why should I have confidence in myself? I paint.

Q: For me security is a sense of being whole.

K: Yes. I did not want to use that word, because then one has to go into the question of what it is to be whole.

Q: But if you feel whole, you are not necessarily self-centred.

K: You see, thought is in itself limited and therefore fragmented. Thought in itself. It is limited, fragmented, and our education cultivates that thinking: 'Have confidence in yourself'; 'You are much better than X', and so on.

Q: Sir, I think we are covering too much of the whole of childhood.

K: All right, sir, let us take one thing. The child comes to you conditioned; conditioned to be afraid, to want security, to want to be like the rest of the gang, violence and all that. He comes to you like that. How will you educate him or help him to be totally different, non-fragmented?

Q: But the child isn't any different from us, because we are that.

K: I know all that, but as an educator, if you are interested in unconditioning, in helping the child to be whole, how will you set about it?

Q: Well, wouldn't one of the first things be to develop an awareness of the conditioning that does exist?

K: How will I be aware of his conditioning and my conditioning? How will I be aware? You see, that is why I do not want to spread it too much. Let's say we have fifteen boys and girls. They come conditioned to be afraid, to want freedom, to have no authority yet wanting authority, wanting to please you, and so on. All that is social, economic, cultural conditioning. And I am also conditioned that way. Then how shall I help them and myself to unravel it, finish with it—if that is what we want? So that they are non-fragmented human beings, so that when they leave us they are whole, not broken up. If that is what we want, what should we do; how shall we go about it?

Q: If you point out the problems inherent in nationality, in separate religions and all of that, surely the next step would be in the sense of self. That is also illusion.

K: They don't know a thing about all that. They don't how to reason, The brain is not sufficiently developed, and so on. So how will you deal with this group of 5 to 12 year olds?

Q: If we start with the feeling of security, surely that is something that comes from the relationship the child has with the teacher.

K: Now what do you mean by security? Let's stick to that one thing. Let's work it out.

Q: It is important.

K: It is important. I feel it is really important. Now, how will you give those 5 to 12 year olds the feeling of complete security?

Q: By being trustworthy yourself, so that you would never betray a child.

K: They do not even know what it means.

Q: But they sense it, they feel it.

K: So how will you have that feeling? Here we are, sir. You and I and a few of us are going to be teachers here. How will you create this?

Q: I would say for the 5 year old the security is part of the whole environment that the child is living in. As he develops, as he grows older, he will have some kind of inner strength that he can work from. And then as the conceptual level develops, he starts to confront things, knowing that he won't be pushed off balance.

K: Sir, which means what? Let's go a little deeper into it. You have a child of 5. You are going to be with him most of the time. You want to create in that child a sense of great trust in you. How will you bring about the feeling that he can rely on you physically, intellectually, morally, spiritually, and have good taste, a sense of appreciation of beauty, all that?

Q: In the early years wouldn't you say that it's the atmosphere that is created, a sense of harmony?

K: How do you create this harmony? The child is there. How do you create it?

Q: Isn't it largely the relationship among the people there that creates it?

K: I want to think of it anew.

Q: I think a child picks up the friendliness, the openness, the relaxation among people faster than an adult.

K: Just a minute. He and I are teachers in that school, but he does not like my taste. He doesn't like my clothes, or my books, my looks, my outlook. How do I, in working with him, bring about an atmosphere to the child? That teacher is far more intellectual than I am. I am slightly romantic, sentimental, and he is not. So there is already, between him and me, a tension, conscious or unconscious. So how do we two create this atmosphere of harmony? We eat together, we talk together but there is an inward feeling of, you know, 'I am more superior than you are'.

Q: Well, surely sensitivity is necessary between the adults.

K: This is a fact I am dealing with.

Q: People's differences should not bring about tension.

K: Ah! So what is it that is bringing him or me or you together for this? I think this has to be separate, a basic thing.

Q: Are you talking about respect? Are you talking about the teacher conveying to the student that he respects him?

K: No. You said just now that there must be harmony. The fact is there is none; and when half a dozen of us are gathered, we are not harmonious. So how do you bring this sense of unity or harmony when in actuality it does not exist? The question is: what has brought us together here, to this school and so on? What has brought us together?

Q: Hopefully it is a common concern for having a school.

K: Ah, be careful, sir. That would mean an idea brought us together.

Q: No, there is no idea. We are just concerned about education.

K: Yes, which means what? You have to go very deeply into this matter if you want to. Do I come to the school as a teacher because it is a conceptual projection? Do I come to Ojai because I believe in what you are doing?

Q: To some degree, Krishnaji. I mean, if you were running a military academy, probably no one would be in this room.

K: Ah, no, I want to state it basically. Otherwise we will go off.

Q: It is the child. You have come for the child. You have come for the children.

K: I am not coming for the child.

Q: Well, you are an educator.

K: No, you see, I want to find out why I come. You say I come for the child. I said I am not sure I have come for the child.

Q: What are you are coming for?

K: We are going to find out. Am I coming for the child? Am I coming because I have no other job?

Q: Sir, we explore these things when someone comes.

K: I am doing it now, sir, not when somebody comes. I am here. I am coming to your school. Why am I coming? If I were a communist, I come to your school because I would make those children into communists.

I am very clear on it. I come here because I see there must be a total psychological revolution in human beings. I mean, we are going to pieces, we are going to die. So I think I would like to begin with the youngest so that they grow. That is what I want. I come here for only that reason.

Q: Can you bring that about, or do you expect someone else to show you how to bring about this revolution?

K: First I must be aware of the world, what is happening in the world, how destructive it is, and so on; and aware that I am part of that world and that any social or political changes can only take place when the world is me and I am changing. That is simple. So, can we say that we are not coming together for an ideal? Do you agree to this so easily?

Q: Does not the psychological revolution itself become an ideal for many of us?

K: No, it is a fact. A fact is never an ideal. That tree is never an ideal; it is a tree. Wait a minute, sir. Just a minute, here it comes. The word *idea* in Greek means to see. The word *idea* means to see—not what we have made up, not I see and then I draw an abstraction from what I see, and that becomes an idea. So, I come without a single ideal. I come only with facts; the fact being that the world has been going around in a certain pattern for millennia and that pattern is destructive, not only to nature but to everything; and unless there is a

profound psychological change in mankind, the thing will...
and so on, so on. That is a fact, it is not an ideal.

Q: When you see that, then there is an urgency, a non-verbal
urgency, for me. It is an urgency.

K: Yes, there is an urgency.

Q: You must find a way to act, and if you do not, you simply go
on in any of the other situations which have not acted on this
problem. That's apparent to me.

K: I want to be clear, sir, that we all see this before we go further; that we are not coming together for an ideal. An ideal
implies something that will take place in the future.

Q: Can one say that one is coming together in a sort of common rejection of something?

K: No, no, I do not reject.

Q: You reject a state in which the world and humanity is...
(inaudible)

Q: Then why do you state something else?

K: I see that to go along that path, you are going to, I don't
know, fall.

Q: Well, isn't that a rejection? Isn't that a turning away from
that?

K: No. I do not turn away. The two have nothing to do with
each other.

Q: Well, they have nothing to do with each other in the working out of it, but as the beginning, the motive, you asked why
one comes to this.

K: Ah, I have no motive.

Q: Well, why then does one start such a school?

K: I am pointing it out. As humanity is going, it is coming to a
precipice, and I see it. Therefore it's finished, I do not go back.

Q: Perhaps rejection implies some sort of conflict you don't intend.

K: It is not rejection.

Q: You have turned away from that path that is leading to disaster.

K: I move away because that is a dangerous. But the moving away is not an idea. Communism, Catholicism, are ideas which have nothing to do with facts.

Q: But does one dare hope that such an environment will change this direction? I mean, it is not an ideal but certainly the hope is there.

K: I have no hope. If you see something dangerous, you leave it, don't you?

Q: In the moment.

K: No, no, you leave it for good—danger is danger!

Q: You leave the danger, not the idea of danger. Is that what you are saying?

K: Of course. I wonder if you are getting this.

Q: You don't leave the idea of a rattlesnake; you leave the rattlesnake.

K: The rattlesnake is not an idea, it is there. I don't say, 'I hope it won't bite me', I just leave, run or something. I think it is a basic thing, sir, which is, do I come to Ojai because I want to carry out an idea which I have? Therefore, idea and the fulfilment of that idea become very important to me; and if you are not of that same idea, there is tension between you and me, which the student or child is going to feel. So I must be very clear that I am not coming for an ideal.

Q: I think this is something terribly fundamental, in the sense that perhaps most of us have what we might call attitudes.

K: No, please, let's stick to this one thing and move from there, otherwise we will go on, round and round. Do I come to it with an ideal, which is non-factual? Ideals are never factual. Factual being that which is.

Q: Do you mean that one should have such fluidity that you do whatever is to be done at the moment, that it arises without...

K: No, madam, I am trying to find out why a group of us come together as teachers at Ojai. If that is not clear, we are going to mess up the thing. Do I come for an ideal? Communists have ideals, Catholics have ideals; human beings generally have some kind of illusory, non-factual images. You may or may not. So am I coming there to fulfil myself or am I coming here to carry out a certain system of education, or am I coming here first because I see very clearly, factually the "despair" that is around me—*despair* in quotes—the degeneration around me? And because I have a son, I say I must save him from ruination. That is my interest. I have no ideal. I say, 'I want that boy to grow so intelligent that he will meet everything as he grows'. So I want to uncondition the boy, from me, from my society, from my culture, all the rot that is going on.

So can we, ten of us or five of us, come here because we only see facts? The fact, the world and so on; the fact that the child must have complete security; the fact, not the idea, that he must be secure.

Q: That basic premise of security is not an ideal?

K: It is not, it is a fact. I must have security, food, clothes and shelter; otherwise my brain goes to pieces. If I do not have proper nourishment, proper clothing and so on, my brain will not function.

Q: Well, the security of food, clothing and shelter is easy to understand.

K: So I come here for factual reasons, not romantic, not imaginary, not sentimental or personal: I come here to see that these children are totally unconditioned, are different. And that means first that I want to give them the feeling that they are completely secure here, physically, intellectually, morally. Now, how do I bring about this feeling of security amongst ourselves as well as the student?

Q: Reasonable boundaries. If you could have reasonable boundaries, that would give a person, especially a young person security.

K: Boundaries where?

Q: Of behaviour and...

K: Ah, ah. Immediately you have boundaries, you have limited action.

Q: Well, you keep expanding them.

K: Which means time, which means the whole idea of progressive and illusionary movement. I'm sorry, I mustn't go off on this. The house is on fire! You don't say, 'Well, let's sit down and talk about it. Who set it on fire, was he a black man, white man, purple man, or yellow man, or bearded man?' We get together and put it out.

So, to come back: can we give ourselves a feeling that we are completely secure here? Shall I go into it? First of all, if you will go into it, is there such thing for grown-up people as security, apart from physical necessities, clothes, food and shelter, which give a certain security? Apart from that, is there such thing as being secure—in my relationships, in my thinking, in my morality, attitudes, conclusions, and so on? I may conclude something, and you come along a minute later and break that up. If I am intelligent, I see your point, I accept your conclusion and break it up. But is there security in any conclusion? Is there security in any relationship: husband, wife, son, daughter, you know, the whole thing? I want security in relationship because without having security in relationship, I feel lost. Or I say, 'All right, I will become negligent, indifferent', I change partners every other day, which is what is happening anyhow.

I do not know if you want to tackle this problem so deeply. Personally, that is the only way for me to attack it and come to it at its greatest depth, not superficially. So, for me, there is no security; therefore there is complete security. And my brain accepts that—not *accepts*, it says, 'That is so. You have sought security there, there, there, there. You are a damn fool, you have not found it. So, is there security anywhere?' And there is not, therefore... (Laughs)

Now, I want to convey that to my son or daughter. They cannot possibly understand this. They say, 'What the... You're a nut!' So I want to convey this, not as an idea, but as a reality, as something as solid as a mountain. How am I to do it? Because the security that man has sought becomes unintelligent. It is unintelligent to be a Catholic, a communist or a Hindu, and so on. So in seeing that there is no security is the act of intelligence, and therefore intelligence is the most complete security. Not intellectually. So I want to convey this to my children. How am I going to do this? Because that is what I want them to find out. I want them to live that way. Not 'I want', that is the only way. So how shall I convey it?

If I were part of the school, part of your staff, I would begin with that question and ask, 'Is this what you and I want, to see that the security man has sought, the things he has invested his whole energy in, are things which are not secure?'

If all of us see that very clearly, then I would say, 'Now, how do we convey this to students aged from 5 to 12?'

May I go on? First, I want the student to listen to me. It does not matter what I say; I want him to listen to me; that is to learn the art of listening. Which he does not have. He is distracted, he is noisy, he is rowdy, restless, playing about. The first thing I want him to learn is how to listen. How will you set about this so that he voluntarily wants to listen to you? How would you do this?

Q: First of all, you have to have something to say.

K: No, no. Sorry. The art of listening, not to what I am saying, which will come later, but he must know what it means to listen. How will you set about it?

Q: Sir, any movement away from his not listening creates a conflict between you and the child.

K: Agreed. Restless, noisy, pulling, mischievous: he is all that. But he must learn the art of listening.

Q: Sir, that is an idea, isn't it?

K: No. You see, you are translating it as an idea. I say, 'Listen', but he won't. So how will he learn to listen, not as an idea? How would you set about it?

You see, he must learn—not *must*; well, all right, I will use the word *must* quickly—learn the art of listening, the art of seeing, the art of learning. Not what to learn, what to see, what to hear, but the capacity, the ability, the interest of listening. Oh, come on, this seems so simple. Move!

Q: He can't be afraid.

K: No, no, I am not concerned with that. He may be afraid. I want him to listen.

Q: Observe?

K: That comes later. First listen. Observe implies seeing. We will go into all that, but learning. First, listening.

Q: Are you implying, sir, that he has to listen without the interference of the mind's preconceptions?

K: Ah, no, you are making it complicated. He must learn the art of listening. When someone says something, he will listen because it is very important to listen. That may be the whole miracle of education. Sorry.

Q: Sir, to listen a child has to be very still, and he is not.

K: Ah, do not say he must be still. I am going to find out. We are learning how to bring about change in a student who is restless, mischievous, noisy, disrespectful, who has never said, 'I must listen'. He hasn't time, he is rushing from here to there, or he is so occupied in drawing something or other. It is necessary that he learns from the very beginning the art of listening.

Q: Sir, when you use the phrase 'the art of listening', do you mean something special by that, or do you mean just listening?

K: The art of listening. It is an art. I am going to find out what it means. It is a tremendous art. So this certain word *art* means to put everything in its right place. Sorry, I am not your teacher, sir! So how shall I help him to listen? To listen to the birds, listen to the waves, to listen to the noise of cars going by, to listen to what I am saying, what you are saying. Listen. How shall I? Because he has never learnt that, because the mother, the father, the parents have no time to tell him to listen. They only tell him to listen when they get angry, irritated. So he blocks it. He blocks, he does not listen. So how shall I help him? Because I think, and you must also think, it is one of the basic, rudimentary, essential things in education. To listen to music. Listen.

Sirs, if you think that is important—not *think*—if you see that is essential, how will you do it? I come to you and say, 'Listen, this is the basic educational thing, the foundation, not "the three R's". These are the basic things: the art of listening, the art of seeing, the art of learning'. And I say to you, 'Work it out'. Now, how do you work it out? You say, 'By Jove, there is truth in that. I want to find out how to do this'. What will you do?

Q: Sir, the phrase 'the art of' disturbs me because it implies that there is a systematic order of learning.

K: No, no, no. Sir, as I said, the boy is rushing, restless, noisy, playing, absorbed in something, and you come along and say, 'Listen'. You want to help him to listen.

Q: I feel that I should listen first to him, keep hearing him.

K: Ah, no, not to him. You are making it so... What has he to tell me? Please, do not complicate this, it is very simple. If we feel it is absolutely essential in education that he should learn just to listen, because you are going to tell him something profound, something true or something false, he must listen to find out. Which means he must have respect for you, he must attend to what you are saying or are going to say. He must have all his energies in listening, to listen, because you may be speaking the absolute truth and if he does not know how to listen, it will just be words. So how do you help the student?

Come on, sirs. I know what I would do. I don't want to tell you because... Come on sirs, work with me.

You want your son to listen to you. You want to tell your son that you love him, and when you say that, he must listen to you, mustn't he? He cannot listen to you when he is chasing a butterfly or is noisy, or playing. You want to tell him, 'I love you', and you want him to listen to that. Listen not to the words but to the depth, the quality of it, the feeling that you have this tremendous feeling of love. How will you help him to listen to you? Because when you say to your son, 'I love you', you mean it tremendously seriously. It isn't a catchword or something casual; you want to tell him this tremendous feeling that you have for him.

Sirs, I was speaking in Bombay. There were seven to eight thousand people there, children too, and they were absolutely silent. They did not even move. I am just telling you, there is nothing personal about it. It happens whether there are two thousand, five thousand or eight thousand, or a few. Why does it happen? Because the speaker is serious when he speaks. So when I say to my son, 'I love you', I am very, very serious. But he has been everlastingly playing, running about till he drops into bed, so he has no occasion to listen. So I must create the occasion for him to listen. I say to him, 'Please, don't play for quarter of an hour, come and sit beside me. Just sit, hold my hand'. So I have created the occasion where he will have the capacity to listen. When I tell him on that occasion that I love him, he knows I mean it. Therefore there is a tremendous rapport. I say to him, 'Now we are going to create an occasion where you are going to sit still and listen'. I would do this before every class. So we create an atmosphere where the student feels, 'By Jove, I must listen'.

After all, that is the beginning of meditation. Meditation is the whole thing we are talking about. And then from there, the art of seeing. I can go on. This is endless.

Sirs, can we do this at Ojai, with all your help? You see, that will cultivate the art of listening, seeing. It is a total thing, not a fragment. It is something whole.

So, is the sermon over?

You have heard this before. There was a teacher who used to preach every morning a sermon to his disciples. One day he got up on the rostrum, and, just as he is about to begin, a bird comes and perches and begins to sing. And they listen to it. After the bird flies away, the teacher says, 'The sermon for this morning is over'.

9

HOW WILL YOU INVITE TRUST?

Questioner (Q): Sir, could we go into the art of learning? A recent survey studying the backgrounds of children who became distinguished academically discovered something similar in their backgrounds. They all studied in very simple places, with small beginnings. Perhaps in talking about learning, we could talk about the environment for learning.

Krishnamurti (K): What does it mean to learn? What is the process of learning? Is it memorizing, accumulating information, accumulating experience of different kinds and different varieties, accumulating knowledge about the universe, about all the things of the universe? Is it a process of accumulation of information, acquiring tremendous knowledge about the "ascent of man", about science, archaeology and so on? I think we ought to find out what it means to learn, don't you? If I am an educator, what am I teaching students? To learn to read and write, sharpen their brains through application, through striving to acquire more and more and more knowledge, so as to be skilful in action in any field they enter? I think it is important to find out what we mean by learning.

And what is the point of learning? To become professors? To become businessmen? To go off to Africa and convert people to Christianity? What is the point of all this enormous striving after learning? Sir, you are going to teach those children. What do you mean by teaching and learning?

Q: It seems to me that at least one kind of learning is what you described, the acquisition of information; and the point of doing that is partly in order to earn a living, and partly just in order to cope with various challenges that life presents.

K: Yes, sir. When you say you are teaching, you are giving them information, are you?

Q: That is certainly part of it.

K: Then what is the other part? Would you say the other part is to understand or learn the whole meaning of life?

So there are two things involved in teaching: to help students to acquire technological knowledge so that they can earn a livelihood in a society which is corrupt, which is degenerating; and also you are teaching them the whole meaning of life. Are these two separate? I am just asking, I am not laying anything down. Are these two separate?

Q: They certainly can be. Most students master the basic academic skills without learning anything about the whole of life.

K: So what is the function of a teacher? What are you teaching? Both? Or are you emphasizing the one and neglecting the other?

Q: Well, it tends to be both. For myself, and I would imagine for most educators, one knows something about the technological side, but when it comes to the wholeness of life, one's understanding is much more limited.

K: Aren't most teachers and educators, whether they are kindergarten or professors in a university, only concerned with the technological side? And even if they teach philosophy, psychology, it is not at all directed to the transformation of man, but only to acquiring knowledge. So it is all the process of gathering knowledge. Is that the function of a teacher? I am just asking. I am questioning it.

The other day we were talking about the art of listening, the art of seeing and the art of learning, and now someone brought up the question of what learning is, the art of learning. We were saying that the function of a teacher, apparently, in the present social structure, is to give students knowledge, technological, psychological, and cosmic, universal; to give them as much knowledge as possible so that they can act skilfully in any vocation they take up. Is that the function of the teacher or educator? There are two problems involved in this: what is learning and what is teaching?

Q: I have heard that there are two views of the teaching situation. One is that the student is empty and the job of the teacher is to fill him up; and the other is that the student already knows everything, only it is all covered over, and then the job is to uncover it, to help the student uncover it. And it seems that those create different teacher roles. In the first case you are pouring more knowledge or information into the empty student. In the other case, it is almost...

K: Awakening?

Q: Yes, a kind of awakening. Our Western education is all based on the teacher filling the student up.

K: That is what is happening in the East too, in India, Japan, in China. Even in the communist world, it is filling the student, so that he can adjust himself to society, compete for the best job, and so on. This is all over the world, at least as far as I know, as far as I have watched it.

Q: You can argue just as well that the child comes into the world a fully conscious being, and then that consciousness gets covered over.

K: But is it true?

Q: For me that idea has a lot of power.

K: Ah, no. Is it factual? It is not what you and I like or dislike. Is it that a child does not need any information, because he is already all there? You are assuming an awful lot, aren't you?

Q: Yes, and I have had a few experiences myself that seem to make it factual for me. But it does assume an awful lot.

K: Sir, sorry. Take someone such as Bach, Mozart or Beethoven. They were tremendous geniuses in their lives. They learned a little bit of technique, but it was all there, bubbling. Is this so with every child? It would be marvellous if it were so.

Q: It would seem to me that what is there is not so much specific knowledge of how to play music, but what is there is a kind of capacity.

K: Ah, you are talking of capacity there in the child, in the student. So would you say the function of the teacher, educator, is to cultivate that capacity to its fullest extent?

Q: Yes.

K: That means the educator must be extraordinarily awake to each student's capacity.

Q: Yes, I would say so.

K: We talked about this in India many years ago. That means having an exceptional educator. He must watch the student, he must have a rapport with him, there must be a relationship of trust from the student, a feeling of great security with the teacher. All that and much more is implied.

Q: Yes, absolutely.

K: So, there is learning, teaching and awakening. That is, teaching implies giving the student information so that he utilizes that information according to his capacity; and awakening that capacity to its greatest extent. For the student to do that, he must feel tremendous security, trust, and have a feeling that you are his mentor, that you are looking after him totally.

So, shall we begin first with whether the educator can establish a relationship with the taught, a relationship of great trust? Can we, at Ojai? How would we proceed? Before we go into that, would you also look at what learning is? Not what you learn *about*—mathematics, geography—but what is the act of learning?

Forgive me, but is there such thing as learning? Learning generally implies accumulation, and from that accumulation you act either skilfully or not so skilfully. I want to question whether learning can ever be accumulated. Then it becomes mechanical, repetitive, leading to boredom and, being bored, to escapism through drink, sex, entertainment, the religions and so on. I want to question if there is a learning which is not accumulative at all.

Q: I see it as a series of realizations.

K: Don't see it yet. Wait, wait—we are just turning the pages over.

Q: Doesn't learning imply something that has happened in the past that is not something real to me now? It has the flavour of something that one has learned and it's there in the background.

K: Education, as it is, is accumulating knowledge and acting according to that. Knowledge, being the past, acts skilfully, and so on. I want to find out if such learning, which is accumulation, is necessary at all. I can learn cycling in about a week, and that becomes a quick habit. I can learn how to drive a car in about a fortnight or so; or learn a language in three months. Those are all accumulative processes. Am I stating things rightly? I cannot suddenly drive a car when I have never been taught.

Q: Well, there is a moment, though, when you know how to drive a car.

K: There is a moment after you have taught me. I can't get into that car and just drive off.

Q: Well, the whole action can be looked at as a series of moments that aren't accumulative.

K: Ah, no, that is a theory. Actually, to learn a language, you have to go through all the business of grammar. You are bombarded with Latin or Greek or Italian, and your brain is so shocked it begins to absorb very quickly.

I want to go into this. I want to question whether learning is necessary at all, apart from technique. If I am to function in the computer business, I must know something about it; I can't just get there and bust up the whole thing. So I must learn; I must watch, listen to what you have to say, and pay tremendous attention to do it immediately. All that means I must acquire some information about it. And the more experience I get in that, the more I begin to invent something new there. Or I may not need experience but suddenly see something about the computer after listening to you. So I must learn some information about it. That is one form of learning. Is there any other learning? Apart from you teaching me architecture, what are you teaching me? I am your student. What are you teaching me?

Q: Well, the way I live my life, the way I approach problems, the way I approach people. That information is all there, I carry it around, I live it, and that is there for the student to see.

K: So you become my example. I don't want you to be an example.

Q: That's fine, you don't have to select it but it's there.

K: No, no, what are you teaching? That is what I want to get at. How to live? Are you teaching me how to live according to your ideas, according to what you have found, according to your responses, your reactions, your way of looking? Are you teaching me all that?

Q: I don't know if I would say I was teaching it to you, but that influence is there and it does come from my ideas, it comes from my conditioning, it comes from my culture. It is all there, and the students see that and may or may not learn it.

K: But I am learning from you, all the same. That is one form of accumulating knowledge. I like you therefore I accept all that you are saying. Why should I learn from you about life, how to live?

Q: I guess it's because none of us really know the answer.

K: No, sir, I want to question, I want to go into it. I want to find out what learning is.

Q: Probably it is not a deliberate process on the part of the teacher. The teacher feels that he is teaching a technique or teaching architecture but in fact he and everything else that is around the student are all contributing to the learning process of the student. The student is also learning from other children.

K: But I am questioning it. I may not want to learn from any of you. I am questioning the learning business itself. You are telling me that I have to learn from you, from many people, not only technical things but also about life according to Jesus, according to the Pope, according to Buddha, according to this or that. So you are all filling me with what you all think, about the way I should live. And I say, 'Why should I? What is this learning? Why should I follow anybody?' I am not vain, but I am questioning it. So I must really find out what it means to learn.

You bring all your own views about how I should live, according to you, according to him, according to the Catholics or the Protestants, communists, and so on. Why should I learn the way I should live? Have you really found out how to live or are you telling me an ideological way of living, according to Christ, according to the Buddha, according to Mao, according to a million people? That is what we have done. The Catholics said, 'Live this way'; the communists have said, 'Live this way'. And I say, 'No, I am sorry, I do not know what you are all talking about because I do not know what it means to learn. What are you teaching me? Words?'

Q: Sir, it is an extraordinary child who goes through this questioning process.

K: No, I am not questioning. No. Let's start. I will not accept any authority. Which doesn't mean I am an anarchist. I will not accept any authority. That means I have no fear of success, failure, all that business. I have no fear. And I have no authority. So I will not follow anybody. I am not being dogmatic about it, I am just pointing out. So what are you teaching me?

Q: There are things that are facts, there are things that are true.

K: Yes, you have taught me facts.

Q: But not just technical facts.

K: What other facts?

Q: For instance, you can point out to a student that he cannot begin from anywhere but where he is. You can point that kind of thing out without being an authority. It does not require them to accept me. They can see that those are facts, that are true. You can deal in that area.

K: Why should you point that out to me?

Q: To help you?

K: I don't want your help. I want to find out. Please, I am not being cantankerous; I want to find out what we mean by learning.

Q: I think many children have a passion for learning.

K: No, I am not talking about children. I want to find out what we grown-up people mean by learning.

Look, I am not being personal; please, forgive me, I am not, really. They sent me to school. I have not learnt a thing from somebody. I have not learned how to look, how to listen, how to be attentive, how to meditate. I have not learnt it from anybody. This is literally so; I do not read books about all these things, I do not learn. Now, I say to myself: here you are, teaching me how to read a book. You are teaching me how to look at facts. So you are all the time guiding me, subtly or crudely or with affection, but you are guiding me. And that may be the curse of our civilization, culture.

Q: Krishnaji, isn't every child, every human being, being exposed to a form of that just by existing? You go down a street and you see something and it makes an imprint on the mind.

K: Wait, wait, wait! So what are you trying to teach me? Are you trying to teach me to keep awake, teach me to be totally aware? Not guide me how to be aware, but just to be aware, to look? Nobody taught me how to be aware.

Q: Yes, but they taught you other things. They taught you how to play golf, they taught you how to speak French, they taught you how do a whole lot of things on that level.

K: That is right. Therefore, we are coming to it: what is learning apart from that? And when you emphasize that, then my mind is crippled or burdened with all that and I am lost. I am caught in that.

Q: Then learning is the ability to find out for yourself.

K: No, look at it the other way. When you educate me, educate a boy or a girl to acquire knowledge so as to live in the world skilfully, intelligently, and the brain is stuffed with that, I am finished, I have no space. And you call that learning. And I say to myself that that is a part of learning, that is learning. But there is a field in which you can never learn anything—learn in the sense of accumulating knowledge and acting according to that. Does it all sound crazy?

Q: Isn't there possibly also an intermediary step between learning techniques and that other learning that you spoke of? Teaching children to say thank you is learning of their relationship with others.

K: No, I am trying to find out what learning is. Is there such a thing as learning at all, apart from that? We are not meeting each other.

Q: Apart from the accumulation of knowledge, is there a learning that is entirely different?

K: I want to say, apart from that there is no learning.

Q: Learning and the accumulation of knowledge are the same?

K: Apart from accumulation of knowledge there is no other learning.

Q: Are you saying that learning is something that comes from the outside and is an influence, has an effect? Is that what you mean in this particular discussion by learning?

K: I have a son. I want him to learn French, Italian, mathematics. Learn. And after learning, accumulating, to live skilfully in that area. And I want to tell him, 'There is no other learning, old boy', so there is no psychological build-up of the "me".

Q: There is no self-knowledge?

K: There is no self-knowledge. Wait a minute, careful. There is self-knowledge in the sense, learning, never accumulating about yourself. I only know myself as knowledge, which is the past; and that past will dictate my learning in the future. So it is not learning, it is adding or subtracting.

Q: Then real learning must be always new.

K: Ah, wait, do not put that in yet. Wait. I want to learn about myself. I know what learning means. You have taught me that it is to accumulate knowledge. So I accumulate knowledge about myself, because I have watched myself in my reactions, my jealousies, my anxieties, my ambitions, my greed, my this and that. So I say, 'Yes, I know up to now what I am'; and when the next year comes, I carry what I have known previously and that knowledge prevents the real understanding of what is happening now, because it is a burden I am carrying. So I am never learning; I am accumulating.

Q: Is there a knowledge which does not accumulate?

K: No, that is what I... There is no knowledge. Don't use that word. Knowledge means acquired information, which is the past; looking from the past and gathering according to the past. And that is what you call learning. And I say that is not learning at all. You are just carrying the burden of yesterday and that is twisting, changing, modifying the present. And so that present is absorbed by the past, modified. So all the time you are modifying, changing, subtracting, adding. That is what knowledge is, what you have done technologically.

So what have I done? I have not learnt about myself, I have only accumulated information about myself: what I am, what I am not, what I should be, what I should not be, and so on. And I say: what is there to learn about myself? I have done this for a period of five years, suppose, and I have learnt so much. I can go on, go on, adding, adding, adding, or taking away little bits. That is not knowing myself. I may be nothing. Oh Lord. You see, sir, does knowledge mean words?

Q: Not for me.

K: What does it mean to you? It means words.

Q: Well, symbols can carry it, can carry the knowledge.

K: Yes, that is the vessel.

Q: But knowledge is the meaning that underlies it. I guess it is how the meaning of a particular event or thing ties into other meanings.

K: Sir, can you say, can anyone say, 'I know my wife', or my husband? The moment you say, 'I know', you are making that person into a dead entity. So when I say I know myself, I am dead.

Q: Yes.

Q: It is not the same thing to say you can know who you are not.

K: That is right. You see, sir, I know how to speak a little bit of French, Italian, Spanish. Right? I know how to drive a car. I know how to write and read. Apart from that I know nothing.

Q: A very simple declaration.

K: Yes. No, no, if you go into that, it becomes very interesting. You see, words... the moment I know nothing, there is only nothingness. And if there is something which is not nothingness, then that something gets attached to what I write, to what I do, how skilful I am, and so all the mischief begins. If there is nothing, I just act: write a letter, talk, or this or that, anything at all; there is nothing. Then what is learning? You understand, sir? I wonder if I am conveying anything at all.

Sir, is there a learning apart from accumulating knowledge? Apart from accumulation—not *knowledge*—let's put it, apart from accumulation? I know that is a yellow shirt because I have been told and I recognize that as yellow because we all agree to call that yellow. That is a learning, learning which is accumulative. Now, I ask myself if there is any other kind of learning at all. I ask myself. I say, 'Yes, that is a Picasso, a Utrillo or a Van Gogh', and so on. I put all that in that category of acquiring knowledge. And is there any other form of learning? What is the function of a teacher or educator if there is no other form of learning except accumulating knowledge? Which is what the present education system is doing, turning out millions and millions of people with specialized knowledge, turning out engineers and scientists like machines on conveyor belts. And if I have a son and I send him to Ojai, I say to myself: what are they teaching him and what is he learning? To be on the conveyor belt? And if I go into it I may have a feeling, it may be irrational, but a feeling that if we only teach him and help him to be nothing, I think we will produce a genius.

Q: How can you help him to be nothing?

K: As we said, the first thing is that he must have complete security and great trust in you and feel that he is protected—not in the sense held, but protected—and therefore has freedom. Can we do that? Provide security and the feeling of trust in which is implied protection—not from animals, not guidance, but protection. And can we provide a sense of great communication, love? Can the parents, the teachers, the trustees do it? That is why the architecture, the building is tremendously important. Isn't it? So when students come, they feel an atmosphere of great shelter, that here are people they can really trust, who are not telling them what to do. Which does not mean you will let them do what they want, but will immediately create the feeling that here are a group of people they can trust, who won't beat them up, verbally or otherwise. Can we do this? We want a whole person, not a divided person.

Now, how do we set about this if you see this to be the truth, not an idea? Actually this *is* the truth. Here we are, we are teachers. What do we do? Let's discuss it.

Q: We avoid dependence. We see that the protection does not turn into dependence.

K: Of course, yes, but what do we do? We start in January, suppose. How do we create this thing?

All of us are involved in this. You cannot do something different from me because if you do something different we would be destroying each other and the student. We must all see the same thing. May I ask respectfully, do you see or feel the importance and the necessity and the urgency of having this total security, total trust, and a feeling that, at last, here are a group of people with whom students can feel at home? At home, not meaning to do what they like, which is what they have been taught, but a home that will provide them with freedom. Can we supply all that?

Q: Sir, I feel that but I do not see the "how" in that. I do not see how you go about it.

K: No, you and I, half a dozen of us are the school. How shall we begin this?

Q: We are doing it here, communicating as we have been, as we will.

K: Yes, but sir, they come conditioned, they come violent, they come with all the ideas: 'Here is a group of people who talk about freedom and I'm jolly well going to do what I like; not attend classes, go climb trees, break windows, anything I want'. Now, what will you do to break down all that, and yet have freedom? Because without that there is no meaning. How will you give him all that? We have talked, we have discussed amongst ourselves, and tomorrow these students come. How shall we receive them? How can we verbally and non-verbally communicate all this to them? It has to be non-verbal first; you cannot begin verbalizing right off. That would be deadly.

Q: It seems to me that we have to do what you are doing. I mean, the child comes, and if you do anything other than what you are doing, then you are structuring the situation because of him.

K: I understand. What are you doing then?

Q: So you do what you are doing.

K: What is that?

Q: In other words, you're building a community, you're working in the garden, you're talking. And the child gets a sense of trust and acceptance.

K: All right, sir, tomorrow morning we are going to meet together in the assembly place. Right? Then what?

Q: I assume that there is some purpose in meeting in an assembly, and you carry that out.

K: You know the purpose of assembly; to meet together, sit quietly, look at each other, get to know each other, and talk and so on. And then what? How do you convey all this to them? Here is a group of people the students can really trust; not the parents, not the neighbours; they do not trust them. Here are people about whom they can really say are looking after them, and so they have trust in you. How would you convey to them that they can trust you?

Q: So you are suggesting that it is possible to convey in just...

K: I am asking you how you do it. If you say you trust them, they will back away and never come near you.

Q: I know how I do it in my classes. I do it by risking. If I open up in a way that is exposing my own vulnerability, then they see that it is safe for them to open up. That seems to work. The students see that I am risking, and therefore they can risk, and we can trust each other and get closer together. How do you do it non-verbally? I know I have a sense that I do this, and I don't know how.

Q: You are asking how to make the child know that he can trust you. Isn't it true that you don't have to do anything in particular?

K: I understand, but how will you invite that trust? He said that he will show how vulnerable he is, that he is quite open to their criticism, open to their suggestions, is not afraid of them, is not trying to put something over on them, is not trying to cajole them to do or not do anything. In the class or during the day, I can convey all that, verbally.

Q: A part of it for me is sharing in their fears, too. I communicate to them that I have a lot of the same fears that they have.

K: Ah, just a minute, sir. If I know that you are like me, how can I trust you?

Q: Well, I can communicate to you that I am untrustworthy, if I'm open about the fact that I can't be trusted.

K: No, but I want to trust you.

Q: I know. You see, we are all untrustworthy.

K: Ah! I understand that but it is absolutely important, essential for the student to trust you. That is why we have the school. It is essential for me, as a student, to say, 'By God, here are a group of people I can trust'.

Q: But if I am hiding the fact...

K: You are putting a tremendous burden on the student.

Q: Well, sir, we are fearful, and to show that to young children, surely that won't make them feel less fearful, would it?

Q: But if we pretend that we are not fearful that's not going to work either.

K: (Laughs) I can smell it miles away. Put it round the other way: what will make a young boy or girl trust you? What do they demand?

Q: Honesty.

K: Honesty. That you mean what you say.

Q: Yes.

K: No. Sir, as a student, I come from a home where I do not trust, where I am suspicious, I am anxious; I may be beaten, criticized. My parents may say, 'Your brother was cleverer than you are, you are stupid', you are this, you are that. So they have cultivated in me a tremendous distrust. They like me because I am their child but there is no... I cannot trust them. I come here with that feeling and there is something in me which says, 'For God's sake, please, I must trust somebody in life'. I come to you with that feeling. The students do not express that; you know unconsciously that this is going on inside. So I come to you, and what do you give me?

Q: Affection. You give affection.

K: No, how do you? I want to trust you.

Q: This does not necessarily have to happen instantly.

K: I don't know. It may happen within a morning or within an hour, or the moment I come in through the door I say, 'By Jove, here is somebody I can trust, that I love'. It is not a question of time. It may happen in the first second or it may happen a week later, but let's leave that part alone.

Q: If the child would sense that he was not being compared to another child, I think that would make him feel greater trust.

K: All right, you are going to not compare, not give him marks, all that. That is understood. I am asking you: I want to trust you. I want to have some shelter, somewhere I can put my head down, and say, 'Thank God!' And you say to yourself: I am going to study him, I am going to be affectionate to him, I must be very honest'. (Laughs)

Q: The only safe thing is not to do anything, because as soon as you try to do something then you are trying to convince him that you are trustworthy and if you are trying to convince him then he will know it is not true.

K: (Laughs) Of course, sir, that is fatal. But will you give me shelter?

Q: Oh yes, shelter, food, I will take care of you, all that.

K: I know all that you will give me. I know all about that because my mother, father, my grandmother have given me that. Can you really give me shelter? That is what I am longing for; not consciously, but deep down that is what I want. I think when you can give me that, I can then grow, I can do something.

Sirs, I was brought up with people who were tremendously authoritarian: "autocracy of the wise is the salvation of the foolish". But they never told me what to do inwardly. Never. They said I must read this, I must do that, and I passed all that; but inwardly, psychologically they never said to me, 'You must be like that'. But I was not with them all the time. But here is a group of students who will be with you for nine or ten months of the year, and [they need] this feeling that they can put their heads on your shoulder when they want to cry.

Q: I feel there would have to be an extraordinary amount of affection, and I don't know if I have that. I wouldn't know how you create that.

K: Ah, I think you are putting a wrong question. That is what I am trying to make you avoid, putting the wrong questions. Sir, do you see the truth that I need shelter, that I come to you for shelter in the big sense, not just food, clothes and a roof, but that I need shelter? If you see that, you have it. The mother in their house says, 'They must have food'. She goes at it, she works for it, cooks. She may do all kinds of other things, but she says, 'They must have food'. Now, do we feel the same thing about trust? Do we feel that they must have it?

The moment the child comes to you, because you have created it he says, 'My God, there it is!' And it is the responsibility, the function of a teacher, to see that the child has it, as the mother sees that the child must have food.

I think if you see the urgency of it, then you create trust. But if you say, 'Now, how shall I help them to trust me?'... (Laughs) You follow?

SOURCES

J. Krishnamurti in dialogue with parents, teachers and trustees in Malibu and Ojai, California.

14919413R00109

Printed in Great Britain
by Amazon.co.uk, Ltd.,
Marston Gate.